You Can Write

You Can Write
A Do-it-yourself Manual

Eamon Murphy

LONGMAN

To my family:
Leola, Siobhan, Ilanna, Aislinn and Alyssa.

Addison Wesley Longman Australia Pty Limited
95 Coventry Street
South Melbourne 3205 Australia

Offices in Sydney, Brisbane and Perth, and
associated companies throughout the world.

Copyright © Addison Wesley Longman Australia Pty Limited 1985

First published 1985
Reprinted 1986, 1987, 1988, 1989, 1990, 1991, 1993, 1995, 1996, 1997, 1999

All rights reserved. Except under the conditions described
in the Copyright Act 1968 of Australia and subsequent
amendments, no part of this publication may be
reproduced, stored in a retrieval system or transmitted in
any form or by any means electronic, mechanical,
photocopying, recording or otherwise, without the prior
permission of the copyright owner.

Cover Illustration Mark Hammond
Designed by Mark Hammond
Set in 11/12.5 Times (Linotron).
Produced by Addison Wesley Longman Australia Pty Limited
Printed in Malaysia, VP

National Library of Australia
Cataloguing-in-Publication data

Murphy, Eamon.
    You can write.

    ISBN 0 582 87238 3.

    1. English language — Composition and exercises.
    I. Title.

808'.042

The
publisher's
policy is to use
**paper manufactured
from sustainable forests**

Contents

Introduction	ix
Acknowledgements	xi
1 Basic Writing Techniques	1
2 Developing an Effective Style	11
3 Planning your Essay	32
4 Organising your Essay	50
5 Paragraphing	65
6 Developing your Argument	73
7 Punctuating	82
8 Trouble Spots	104
9 Referencing Skills	125
10 Book Reviews	148
Further Reading	155

Introduction

This is a manual for anybody who wishes to improve his or her ability to write well. It is designed to help you — the reader — to write more easily, more effectively and more confidently. Although I initially wrote this for undergraduates and upper-secondary students, much of the material can also be successfully used by others. Teachers whose own writing skills are rusty may find useful hints; the tutors who have already used this as a text have found that their own skills have sharpened. People in the workforce who wish to improve their writing skills can also profitably use this manual. After all, the principles of good writing — clarity, conciseness and accuracy — are fundamental to all writing. Writing up a science experiment, a history essay or a business report all require the common basic skills that this manual discusses.

Over the past few years, the level of literacy of school-leavers has worried parents, teachers, academics and employers. While some of this concern is ill-founded, many students are leaving school unable to communicate their thoughts effectively on paper. Their inability to write clearly seriously handicaps them in the workplace and in further studies. Much time and effort, and many opportunities, are wasted when students lack basic writing skills.

Yet, given training and practice, anybody can write clear, direct and effective English. It is true that some people will naturally write more easily than others; these are the minority — they are lucky enough to have a gift for writing. But you don't need any special gifts to communicate effectively on paper, whether at school, university or work. There is nothing mysterious about good writing.

When writing this manual, I myself have tried to follow the principles of good writing; that is, writing as simply, clearly and directly as possible. I have also made the manual as practical as possible. For instance, many of the examples that I have used come from actual student writing.

As the title says, this is a do-it-yourself manual. To get maximum benefit from it, you should do all the exercises in the spaces provided and check your answers. Underlining or highlighting important points will also help you understand and remember better. I have carefully graded the steps and have provided a detailed commentary on the many examples and exercises. The manual, therefore, is self-explanatory and has been designed for students to work through on their own. It has also been used successfully as a classroom text. Students working through the examples as members of a class or a small group can share their ideas and help one another. The teacher or tutor can easily obtain additional examples from books, newspapers and students' work if necessary.

A draft of the manual has been used with over 300 students at the Western Australian Institute of Technology, and I have revised it to take account of their criticisms and suggestions, as well as those of their tutors. It has, therefore, already been tested and proved in a real teaching situation. I substantially revised it again to take account of the editor's suggestions.

Let's now start by discussing how successful writers go about organising their ideas and information, and how they communicate them effectively in writing.

Acknowledgements

It is impossible for me to name individually all the people who helped me, either directly or indirectly, to write this manual. My thanks to the many students who have stimulated me during the very happy years I have taught in the Department of Social Sciences, Western Australian Institute of Technology. My colleagues at WAIT have also supported and encouraged me through these years. Bruce Ridley of the School of English provided me with the examples of student work that I have used in the text. Carole Duffill of the Robertson Library constructively criticised the sections on using the library. Bill Cooper, Barbara Dobson, Hilton Lague, Peter Turner, Paul Hetherington and Roger Woods made many useful suggestions, which have found their way into the text.

My very special thanks to the following:
Mrs Faye Velickovski and Mrs Sue Plummer for patiently and accurately typing a difficult manuscript; without their assistance, this manual would still be a long way from completion. John McGuire and Will Christensen of the Department of Social Sciences WAIT for their encouragement, support and suggestions. Hugh Owen, my doctoral supervisor at the University of Western Australia, who taught me how to write academic essays. Ray Bailey of the School of English, WAIT, for his patience and time in helping me overcome my own weaknesses in basic English. I owe a great deal to Vivienne Dickson of Longman Cheshire for her painstaking editing, constructive criticisms and valuable suggestions.

Finally, without the love, encouragement and assistance of my wife, Leola, this manual would never have been written.

1 Basic Writing Techniques

Let's get one thing very clear at the start: writing is not an automatic process — **Writing is a learned skill.** People who write well have had to learn to write well. As with any other skill (such as golf), your writing will improve with practice. But it will almost certainly improve much more quickly if you master basic writing techniques. (Likewise, you may become a good golfer simply by playing golf, but the chances are that you will learn to play much better golf, more quickly and with less effort, if you first learn basic golf techniques.) Most people who claim that they can't write, or that they hate writing, have never learnt how to write.

The writing techniques set out in this manual have been successfully used both by inexperienced and professional writers. Adapt them to suit yourself, if necessary. Remember again that being able to write well is not a gift most of us are born with, nor is it a question of good luck. Learn the techniques, practise and you will succeed. With success will come confidence. Once you gain confidence, your writing will improve rapidly. **Anybody can write! You can write!**

Why write?

Ideally, you write because you have something to say — you wish to communicate on paper with another human being. Very little writing is done for the writer's eyes only. This communication may involve feelings and emotions (a poem, a love letter), may provide facts and information (a physics text book, a job application) or may try to convince the reader through logical argument (a history essay, a company report recommending a course of action). Writing may, therefore, (amongst other things) describe, explain, instruct, recommend or persuade. (You may even write because you enjoy writing! Writing may be hard work at times, but it can also be fun.)

But there are at least two very practical reasons why you should (must?) learn to write well: as a student, your ability to write may very well determine whether you will be successful or not. This is particularly so in the humanities and social sciences, but the physical sciences, business studies and other subjects that emphasise factual information also require competent writing skills. Almost all tertiary courses require students to write essays, reports or summaries.

The second reason for learning to write well is that progress in your professional career may very well be determined by your ability to communicate effectively on paper. All other things being equal, the engineer who can impart knowledge concisely, accurately and clearly in writing will make progress in his or her career much more rapidly than an illiterate colleague. The same is true of other professions.

Whatever you write (a letter, essay, book review, report) you will have to think about:

- *why* you are writing — your purpose in writing
- *for whom* you are writing — your audience
- the *best way* of writing — to achieve your purpose and satisfy your audience.

A systematic approach to writing

The following twelve steps will help you develop a systematic, effective, professional approach to writing.

1 Identify your aim

What are you trying to achieve?
Is it:

- to develop an argument?
- to describe a process or event?

- to recommend a course of action?
- to evaluate?
- to provide information?

Before you start preparing to write, finish this sentence:

> My main aim in writing this is to . . . .

2 Identify your audience

For whom are you writing?

- your fellow students?
- a lecturer or tutor?
- a prospective employer?
- a company manager?
- a government committee?

You write alone but, in most cases, you write for somebody else. A real person is at the other end: you must always keep that in mind. To write effectively, therefore, you must consider your reader's needs.

You need to determine:

- How much does your reader know already?
- How much does he or she need to know?
- What is the best writing form to use?

Unless you identify your audience's needs and expectations, you will have great difficulty in writing anything at all. Tertiary students, in particular, have great difficulty in working out at what level they should aim, what approach they should take, or how much background information they should provide. If the lecturer or tutor does not make clear what is expected, assume that your reader is a fellow student who has a general knowledge of the subject. On the other hand, many employers claim that new employees who have come straight from school or university often write as if they are trying to impress a teacher or tutor: they use unnecessarily complicated sentences, provide too many details, and don't get to the point.

Remember always to identify your audience and his or her needs.

3 Plan

You will find it difficult — if not impossible — to write, and your finished work will be disorganised, if you don't plan, that is, develop some sort of outline. There are many approaches you can use when planning. The simplest and often the most effective (especially if you have only to write a short piece) is to list the main points you want to make on a piece of paper, leaving plenty of room for changes. Under each main point you then list subsidiary points. You may find it convenient to use numerals and subnumerals to list your main and subsidiary points. Some writers find it best if they jot each main idea on a separate card so that they can shuffle them around. An outline is not fixed: you may have to experiment with it by rearranging the order or eliminating or listing new points. The outline provides the framework; without it you may quickly get lost.

4 Give yourself lots of room

Write on one side of the paper only, leave wide margins and at least a double space between lines. This is very important. You will need plenty of room later when you come to revise your writing. You may need to cut up and paste, to insert phrases and sentences, to cross out sections. Paper is cheap; your time is precious.

5 Start writing immediately

You may wish to write a very rough introduction, or you may leave your introduction until later. Don't try to write the perfect beginning, or you'll never make progress. Often you won't know exactly what you want to put in your introduction until you have written a first draft. A blank page terrifies some writers, so the sooner you get something down, the better you will feel.

6 Write quickly

Don't worry about neatness, spelling or grammar at this early stage. Many students fall into the trap of trying to write a perfect copy first time. You can't! Very, very few writers can. (Of course, some writers can write quite good English at the first attempt, but most can't.) Writing very slowly and carefully on your first draft can be dangerous. Some of your ideas will almost certainly change, and you will want to make alterations when you have written a draft. If you try to be perfect first time, you will not leave yourself enough time to make changes later. Trying to be perfect first time will almost certainly make you timid and afraid to write anything at all.

7 Write a complete draft, a substantial portion, or a whole section at one go

The first draft is written for yourself; while you don't entirely forget about your reader, don't worry about how it looks or reads at this early stage. Once you've got something down, you've overcome one of the writer's greatest obstacles: getting started. Simply sitting with a pen in hand waiting for a flash of enlightenment will achieve nothing. Instead, it will waste your time, increase your anxiety and still leave you with a blank page to fill. Once you have something written, and you have something concrete to work on, you will automatically start sifting, organising and rearranging. There is some complex psychological explanation for this, but that's not important:

the important fact is that for students, as well as more experienced authors, once you have something written, half the battle is over. You've made the breakthrough. If necessary, break a long piece of writing into more manageable shorter units. You will then have a sense of satisfaction as you complete each. If you try to do too much at one writing session, you may end by being discouraged. You need to feel that you're making progress.

8 Read the entire draft quickly. Make rough corrections, and then leave it for a day or two

You will need to distance yourself from your writing in order to see the mistakes and what needs changing. You can't do it immediately you have written something: at that stage, you can see only what you *want* to see, not what is *actually there*.

9 Revise

Most inexperienced writers do not spend enough time revising; *the best writers revise the most*. What seems like natural writing is usually the result of much revision. If you get a first draft written quickly, as suggested in points 5, 6 and 7 above, you will have time for revision.

Revising consists of two main processes:

Reorganising the structure

The structure may only require minor changes, but you should be prepared to make more substantial changes if necessary. You may want to cut out or add new sections or even chapters of a larger work. Use scissors and sticky tape (or glue) to rearrange paragraphs or parts of a paragraph. Don't worry if it looks a terrible mess.

Polishing up your style

At this late stage in your writing, you must start putting yourself in your reader's shoes. Your aim now is to revise your writing so as to help your reader as much as possible.

Ensure that your writing is easy to read and to understand. Make sure all paragraphs are linked. Each paragraph should deal with one topic. Rewrite long, rambling, awkward sentences. Cut out unnecessary or pompous words and phrases. Check grammar, spelling and punctuation. (I'll deal with these revision and polishing skills later in the manual.) Use standard proofreading symbols to help you revise (see end of this chapter).

10 Give your draft to somebody else to read

Find somebody who will not be afraid to criticise, but won't destroy your confidence. Most writers (including myself) find it hard at first to accept criticism, although all of us can benefit from it. We feel resentful and on the defensive. Writing is, after all, a very personal exercise: we invest a lot of time and energy in it. However, your writing will quickly improve if you open your mind and learn from constructive criticism. If somebody takes the trouble to comment thoroughly on your writing, then regard it as a compliment and learn from it. Being ready to accept criticism (so long as it's fair) requires maturity and some courage, but your writing will soon show the benefit.

11 Final polish

12 Write or type the final draft

Note: If you can get access to a word processor, you will save yourself a great deal of time and effort. Revision is very simple.

Don't expect to become a polished writer in a hurry. If you expect perfection, you will be bound to be frustrated. Too high expectations will destroy your confidence: you will dither around and write nothing. Aim to improve gradually. Build up your confidence. Take pride in even quite small achievements. And, of course, some kinds of writing do not require as much polish as others. For example, many (not all) kinds of business memos can be written straight off.

Other kinds of writing can be more demanding. The amount of effort you put in will depend upon for whom you are writing, what you are writing, your aims in writing, and how much time you have.

Keep in mind also that for most people writing is, at times, difficult and frustrating. It can also be very messy, confusing and depressing. Writing that seems to flow effortlessly is often, in fact, the product of many hours' work. Professional writers will agonise for hours over a sentence. Most people simply haven't the time — or skills — to do this. Inevitably much of your writing will be done under pressure. Some people, in fact, write best when near a deadline. Despite the best intentions in the world, most students find themselves at times having to write at the last minute. But while most writing involves some sort of compromise between deadlines and a desire for improvement, if you want to improve, you will need to leave time for revision.

If you develop a systematic approach to writing, such as the one I've suggested above, you will write more easily with less effort. A writing system will give you an organised way of doing things so that you not only use your time effectively but can also overcome the unexpected obstacles that you (like any other writer) will sometimes meet. A system removes much of the uncertainty, irritation and frustration that all inexperienced writers face.

How to overcome a writing block

Everybody occasionally has a writing block when nothing seems to come out. But you can overcome the block. The following suggestions may help you:

- Get into a routine. Discipline yourself. Even the very best writers go through stages when they feel that they can't write.
- Plan thoroughly. Prepare an outline. It may help if you read further, so long as you don't use reading and notetaking as an excuse not to write.
- Get something down quickly on paper and keep your

Basic Writing Techniques

writing moving — especially the first draft. This is crucial for most writers.
- Break your writing into manageable units. Write in shorter bursts until you gain confidence and experience. Reward yourself when you have achieved your goal.
- Write where you won't be disturbed. You need uninterrupted time to get anything worthwhile done.
- Be prepared to eliminate sections of your writing if necessary. Writers often find it hard to discard sections, but if they turn out to be irrelevant, or not as good as you first thought, they must go.
- Try leaving your writing for a while, perhaps overnight. Don't, however, do this too often. You should not get into the habit of putting off writing. Eventually you will have to face up to it. Do it on your terms. Often a long jog or walk by yourself will help you think through a problem.
- Remember that everybody has the same problem sometimes. **You Can Write**.

Proofreading symbols

When you are revising, try using some of the standard proofreading symbols so you can make changes easily without creating a mess. If your work is typed by somebody else, there will be much less chance of confusion.

Symbol	Example	Stands for
⊢——⊣	~~English~~	delete word
⌒	Englis⌒h	delete letter
⊙	Englis⊙h	change to full-stop
≡	english	capital letter
○	E(N)glish	small letter
∽	E⌣g⌢lish	transpose letter or word

You Can Write

Symbol	Example	Stands for
. . . .	E n g l i s h	let it stand (i.e., ignore the change)
¶	¶English	new paragraph
⌒	English⌒	run-on (not a fresh line or paragraph)

This edited piece:

~~In order~~ to ~~keep~~ *make* their ~~writing~~ *changes* clear, authors ~~make~~ use ~~of a number of~~ proofreading symbols. ~~Despite the fact that~~ there are many more Symbols, *but* most are needed not by the ordinary writer.

Will be typed as:

To make their changes clear, authors use proofreading symbols. There are many more symbols, but most are not needed by the ordinary writer.

Now let's consider how to make your writing more effective.

2 Developing an Effective Style

Writing is work! Make no mistake about it. But it doesn't have to be boring or frustrating. What frustrates many people who want to — or have to — write is that they have no idea how to start, or what they are doing wrong, or why they can't write, or how they can improve. This manual will help you, particularly if you are one of these individuals, whether you're at school, attending university or college, or working in a trade or profession.
   Let's begin.
   To write effectively you need to:

- Know the **principles** of **good writing**. If you don't know what you're aiming at, how can you possibly achieve it?
- Learn **basic writing techniques** — the 'tricks of the trade' — such as how to take notes, organise your material, overcome writing 'blocks' and other difficulties.
- Learn some **basic mechanical skills**, such as punctuation, referencing.

Once you have learnt the principles, techniques and skills, you will soon develop **confidence. Confidence** and **practice** will soon turn you into a good writer.

First, we need to know what the principles of good writing are.
Good writing is clear, direct writing. Good writing results in good communication. Your objective is to get the ideas in your mind into the mind of your reader as effectively as you can. You will learn in time, I hope, to appreciate the richness, complexity and beauty of the English language. But this can wait. You must first of all learn **clarity. Clarity** means clearness; precision of expression; lucidity. It is the opposite of looseness, sloppiness, imprecision. Clarity in

11

writing depends on the use of the right words in the right way so that they clearly convey what is in *your* mind to the mind of *your* reader. That is not to say that your ultimate goal is to reduce all your writing to a very basic level; hopefully, you will learn to take pleasure in experimenting with your style and, ideally, you should in time develop a writing style that clearly carries your message but which also interests and gives pleasure to your reader. But your most important goal now is to learn how to write **clearly** and **effectively**.

Look at these examples. Which do you consider are the better examples of good writing?

a It is considered by this writer that the siting of a manufacturing plant in close proximity to the metropolis will have a detrimental effect on the environment.

or

b I consider that building a factory close to the city will damage the environment.

a Management of this firm has recently become cognisant of the necessity of eliminating the unwanted vegetation which has invaded the periphery of our complex, and urges all staff to make every effort to eliminate same.

or

b The management requests staff to kill the weeds around the building.

a The author of this paper considers that the concept of class is undoubtedly a most useful heuristic device to aid the analysis of societies which have reached an advanced stage of capitalist development.

or

b The concept of class is useful in analysing advanced capitalist societies.

a Company operations for the preceding annual accounting period terminated with a substantial unfavourable deficit.

or

b The company lost a lot of money last year.

Developing an Effective Style

Many people, especially new students at tertiary institutions, would have selected the (a) examples. Why? Perhaps they seem somehow more impressive. But your main goal is not to impress readers with your vocabulary: it is to impress them with the quality of your thinking. And to do that, you must **communicate**. Get rid of words that confuse or irritate the reader.

Unfortunately, you will come across many examples of the opposite. Some academics, scientists, civil servants and other professionals write long-winded, confusing and pompous prose. Such writers mistake obscurity for profundity.

Why do so many students, academics and other professionals adopt a woolly, confusing and difficult style?

Inexperience

Many people are uneasy about using a simple, clear, direct style: they fear they will be ridiculed or ignored by their tutor or employer if they don't use flowery, elaborate sentences and big words and pompous phrases. They forget, or don't realise, that writing — especially scientific, technical, business and academic — has one aim: to communicate. The reader appreciates a writing style that does not get in the way of effective communication. If you have something worth writing, then don't be afraid to write clearly. Students often think that because they are enrolled in a tertiary institution, they must develop an 'intellectual' style, whatever that means. Unfortunately, a minority of academics also confuse simplicity with shallowness, profundity with pomposity.

Laziness

A heavy, pompous style is often used to hide the fact that the writer is not really clear about what he or she wants to say. If you can express your ideas simply, then you really know your subject. Some writers attempt to disguise their lack of preparation or understanding by using big words and very complex sentences to create a smoke-screen.

Game-playing

Writers often cultivate a difficult style to frighten or browbeat the readers, believing the readers will be so impressed by the **way** it is written that they will be afraid to look closely at **what** is written. What actually happens, of course, is that readers either get angry or fall asleep. People who are feeling insecure, such as new students or new employees, often write badly because they want to impress. Civil servants sometimes write in a roundabout fashion to confuse rather than inform. Some academics also write badly. Take this actual example from a draft of an academic book:

> This strategem enabled him to minimise expenditure on the strike by delimiting the financial cost of maintaining each striker.

What does this mean?
 I don't know! The editor didn't know! Probably the academic who wrote this didn't know!

Misdirected teaching

Many scientists, engineers and businessmen associate writing with writing stories and poems, often the only kind of formal writing they were taught at school. They consider that writing is only about emotions, impressions and style and is therefore of little concern to the practical man of the scientific or business world. In fact, the best writing is disciplined, organised and logical: the scientist's professional training often makes her or him an excellent logical, clear and organised writer. Scientists, engineers and businessmen need to be able to write just as much as do teachers, social workers and civil servants.

Poor organisation
Many reluctant writers are unsystematic in their approach to writing, which results in disorganised student essays and incomprehensible reports.

Finding enough words — padding
Many first-year undergraduate students panic when faced for the first time with the task of writing 1500–2000 words. One way they think they can get around the problem is to write loosely, to string out their words ('due to the fact that' instead of 'because'). If you plan properly (as this manual will show you how to), finding enough words will never be a problem; you will, in fact, need to develop the skills to write concisely.

How to develop a clear, effective style

- Learn a few basic principles.
- Gain the confidence to become critical of your own and other people's writing.
- Practise, practise, practise.

Five principles of clear, concise, effective writing

(These are not 'rules'; they are suggestions as to how you can get rid of unnecessary words. In time, you will do this naturally.)

Principle number one: generally keep sentences short and simple

The most common characteristic of bad writing is unnecessarily long, complex sentences. Long sentences may be both necessary and pleasing, but they are often neither.

You Can Write

Long sentences make it difficult for your reader to understand what you have written. In inexperienced or careless hands, very long sentences may:

- overtax the reader's memory
- cause the reader to lose interest and concentration
- irritate and bore
- lose the main point within a jungle of words
- mix up two or more main points
- result in grammatical errors.

This very long sentence is totally confusing:

> Also contribution to precipitation in Southeast Asia and bringing occasional but fairly continuous rainfall for five to seven hours at a time are eastward-moving non-portal storms in the trade wind belt between 80 and 150 kilometres wide, which are linked to upper air fluctuations breaching the inversion layer and thus negating its normal inhibitory effect upon the vertical movement of trade wind air.

Breaking it up into shorter sentences makes it easy to understand:

> Occasional non-portal storms associated with migrating disturbances in the trade wind belt also contribute to precipitation in Southeast Asia. These eastward-moving waves are linked to upper air fluctuations which breach the inversion layer, thus permitting the vertical movement of trade wind air. Between 80 and 150 kilometres wide, they bring fairly continuous rainfall for five to seven hours.

I am not suggesting that your writing should consist of a series of very short sentences. This would make for boring and ineffective communication. Very short sentences are best kept for new, complex information or to create a special effect. And you should, in fact, vary the length of your sentences for variety, emphasis and impact. However, look very carefully at any sentence that seems very long and, if in doubt, reduce its length. If you are not a confident writer, you should start with shorter sentences.

Developing an Effective Style

You will develop your style — your own unique way of expressing yourself — once you gain confidence. Remember that short sentences are much easier to write and to understand. Again, there is no rule about this, and some students will naturally, and quite correctly, write longer sentences than other students.

Take an actual example from a second-year student's essay:

> Numbering about thirty-eight millions, Indian tribals were traditionally hunters and gatherers who, in recent times, have been drawn into the mainstream of Indian society as peasants and agricultural labourers, and, in the process, they have been subjected to much oppression and exploitation, despite legislation enacted for their protection, and despite periodic rebellions, which the British crushed with great violence.

While this is grammatically correct, the two main ideas (the assimilation of tribals and their exploitation) have been rather lost. Very long sentences are dangerous: they can easily confuse the reader, and they can lead to mistakes. One simple remedy would be to break up the long sentence into two or more shorter ones.

Your version:

....
....
....
....
....
....

My version:

> Numbering about thirty-eight millions, Indian tribals were traditionally hunters and gatherers. In recent times, they have been drawn into the mainstream of Indian society as peasants and agricultural labourers. In the process, they have been subjected to much oppression and exploitation. They have

You Can Write

> remained one of the most oppressed sections of Indian society, despite legislation enacted for their protection, and despite periodic rebellions, which the British crushed with great violence.

And then make a further revision such as this:

Edited version:

Numbering about thirty-eight million, Indian tribals were traditionally hunters and gatherers. But in recent times, the tribals have been drawn into the mainstream of Indian society as peasants and agricultural labourers. In the process, they have been subjected to much oppression and exploitation. They have remained one of the most oppressed sections of Indian society, despite legislation enacted for their protection, and despite periodic rebellions, which the British crushed with great violence.

Indian tribals were traditionally hunters and gatherers. But in recent times, the thirty-eight million tribals have been

Developing an Effective Style

drawn into the mainstream of Indian society as peasants and agricultural labourers. In the process, they have been subjected to much oppression and exploitation. Despite legislation enacted for their protection, and despite periodic rebellions (which the British crushed with great violence), they have remained one of the most oppressed sections of Indian society.

The topic of the paragraph is now firmly established in the first sentence with the shifting of the less important information (the number of tribals) to the next sentence. The final sentence is more effective, because the emphasis is now on the last, and most important, point — their continued oppression.
Much clearer?

As you develop your writing skills and, in particular, your ability to punctuate correctly, you can more confidently experiment with writing longer, more complicated sentences. At this stage, however, you should look very critically at any sentence that seems to go on for ever.

Try rewriting this long, complicated sentence:

> In the tenth century the Straits of Malacca were an important trade route in Southeast Asia which in all probability was still controlled by the Hindu Sriwijaya empire, but as the ship traffic and trade communications conducted by the Muslims increased gradually, a permanent Muslim settlement was conducted along the Indonesian coast, as the discovery of a gravestone of a Muslim ruler has demonstrated.

19

You Can Write

Your version:

A possibility:

In the tenth century, the Straits of Malacca were an important trade route in Southeast Asia. At that time, the Hindu Sriwijaya empire probably still controlled the route. However, the recent discovery of a Muslim ruler's gravestone has suggested that, as they gradually increased their ship traffic and trade communications, they established a permanent Muslim settlement.

Developing an Effective Style

You have, of course, an almost infinite number of options. You may prefer, for example, to join the first two sentences.

> In the tenth century, the Straits of Malacca were an important Southeast Asian trade route, probably still controlled by the Hindu Sriwijaya empire.

There is no one correct way of writing anything. Develop a critical sense of what is good writing, then **practise**.

Principle number two: write in the active rather than the passive voice

The passive form (it was said by John that. . .) is grammatically correct, but the active (John said . . .) is clearer, more direct, more concise and more vigorous. Unfortunately, many students imitate those academics and others who consider that the passive voice is more 'scholarly' or more 'scientific'. 'The author of this paper considers that . . .' is in some unexplained way considered more objective and better suited to academic writing than, 'I consider that . . .'. (You may well come across the academic who forbids you to use the 'I' in essays. If you do, then you will have to decide whether you will humour him or her.)

Try rewriting the sentences in the active voice. Count the number of words that you save. (N.B. sentences containing 'by' are often — though not always — written in the passive.)

1 It was stated *by* Brown that Irishmen make excellent immigrants.
   ....

2 He was invited *by* the school to address the children.
   ....

3 Public nudity is prohibited *by* law in all Australian states.
   ....

You Can Write

4 It was suggested *by* the authors of the report that marriage is still very popular among young Australians.

5 The work must be submitted on time *by* you.

6 It was the expectation of the student that she would be awarded a higher mark *by* the lecturer.

7 The experiment was conducted by the engineer.

8 The responses were measured on a computer-controlled device.

9 The car was tested by the automobile club and was found to return a consistently high mileage.

10 The solution was titrated in the flask by the chemist.

Possible active alternatives:
1 Brown stated that Irishmen make excellent immigrants.
2 The school invited him to address the children.
3 All Australian states prohibit public nudity.
4 The authors of the report (*or* the report's authors) suggested that marriage is still popular among young Australians.
5 You must submit your work on time.
6 The student expected a higher mark from the lecturer.
7 The engineer conducted the experiment.
8 A computer-controlled device measured the responses.
9 The automobile club tested the car and found that it returned a consistently high mileage. *or* In the automobile club tests, the car returned a consistently high mileage.
10 The chemist titrated the solution in the flask.

Remember, however, that you will sometimes be quite justified in using the passive. For example, you may wish to retain the passive form in example 3 to emphasise *public nudity*. You may also use the passive for variety. But if you

Developing an Effective Style

overuse the passive, your writing will be dull and stodgy. Moreover, your reader may assume that you are afraid to state your opinion directly.

Principle number three: choose short, familiar words rather than long, unfamiliar words

This does not mean that you should never use a long word. There will be many instances when you will be perfectly justified in doing so. For example, you will find that most academic subjects use long words that have a very specific meaning, and which you cannot avoid using (e.g. 'ethnocentrism' in anthropology). You also may feel that a longer word conveys the meaning most effectively, or — very occasionally — you may use a particular long word because you happen to like it. However, don't use long words simply to impress your reader or, worse still, to hide the fact that you don't know what you're writing about. Too many long, strange words will suggest that you are ignorant or pompous, or both.

> The antiquated mechanisms are only utilised now in the hyperbarean section of the continent.
>
> *which simply means*
>
> The old machines are only used now in the extreme north of the continent.

If a long word helps you communicate better, then by all means use it. If not, look for an alternative.

Fill in the blanks:

Big word	**Equivalent small word**
1 assistance	....
2 commence	....
3 consign	....
4 obfuscate	....
5 facilitate	....
6 terminate	....

You Can Write

7 corpulent ....
8 configuration ....
9 be cognisant ....
10 elucidate ....
11 ascertain ....
12 utilise ....

(*Possible alternatives* — help, begin, send, confuse, help, end, fat, shape, know, clarify, find out, use)

Principle number four: cut out unnecessary words and groups of words

Use no more words than are necessary to communicate effectively. Do not, however, leave out essential information to save words. Distinguish between concision and brevity: **concise** writing contains no unnecessary words; **brief** writing uses only a few words.

Concise writing may also be brief, but not always. There is no point in being brief if the essential meaning is lost; if in your desire to be brief, you leave out important information. While brevity is desirable, **clarity** and **meaning** are the major goals.

You will probably never eliminate all unnecessary words, but the following hints may help you prune the excess. Remember, if you plan your essay carefully, you will not need to scratch around to find enough words. Watch out in particular for **tautology** — unnecessary repetition:

> The chemicals were too few in number.
> ('few' means 'a small number')
> She gave him a verbal tongue-lashing.
> He intends to make a religious film about the bible.

Some examples. Fill in the blanks:

1 **Not**: at this point of time (a current favourite)
  But: ....
2 **Not**: due to the fact that
  But: ....

Developing an Effective Style

3 Not in the near future
 But: ....
4 Not: He is the person who works hard.
 But: ....
5 Not: The wall is green in colour.
 But: ....
6 Not: Personally, I support the Liberal Party.
 But: ....
7 Not: They spoke in a private fashion.
 But: ....
8 Not: I want to make the acquaintance of the young lady.
 But: ....
9 Not: Notwithstanding the fact that the profits were low, the manager was optimistic.
 But: ....
10 Not: The risk is of considerable magnitude.
 But: ....
11 Not: The first beginnings of space travel involved great risks.
 But: ....
12 Not: Oxygen is the vital essential for life.
 But: ....

Answers:
1 now.   2 because.   3 soon.   4 He works hard.   5 The wall is green.   6 I support the Liberal Party.   7 They spoke privately.   8 I want to meet the young lady.   9 Although the profits were low, the manager was optimisitic.   10 The risk is considerable.   11 The beginning of space travel involved great risks.   12 Oxygen is essential for life.

Be especially careful when you use the following, as they are often (not always) part of a loose construction. They are not necessarily wrong; sometimes you will need to use them. Just be cautious.

Note how often 'is' and 'was' appear in these examples.

Watch out most particularly for the verb [to be] and its parts [is] and [was].

1 Not: He *is* sick and *is* in hospital.
 But: ....

25

You Can Write

2 Not: He seems *to be* upset.
But: ....

Other words to watch out for:

[There]

3 Not: *There* was something strange.
But: ....
4 Not: *There* are a number of examples that support his thesis.
But: ....
5 Not: *There* are many women who never marry.
But: ....

[It]

6 Not: *It* is his last book that is his best.
But: ....
7 Not: *It* is probable that this information would help.
But: ....

[Which or that]

8 Not: A train *that* is moving is difficult to halt.
But: ....
9 Not: The research *that* he did on enzymes was important.
But: ....

[Who]

10 Not: The man *who* was sick died.
But: ....

Answers:
1 He is sick in hospital. 2 He seems upset. 3 Something was strange. 4 A number of examples support his thesis. 5 Many women never marry. 6 His last book is his best. 7 This information would probably help. 8 A moving train is difficult to halt. 9 His research on enzymes (or enzyme research) was important. 10 The sick man died.

Developing an Effective Style

Principle number five: change nouns (naming words) to verbs (doing words) wherever possible

Poor scientific writing often overuses nouns. This helps account for the heavy, dull style of some scientific, especially medical, publications.

1 **Not:** Measurement (noun) of the surface area was performed by the device.

   But: ....

2 **Not:** The identification (noun) of the substances is by the use of a colour code.

   But: ....

3 **Not:** The reason for this increase (noun) in muscular strength was due to exercise.

   But: ....

4 **Not:** The article is a summary (noun) of the problem.

   But: ....

5 **Not:** The grant was a stimulus (noun) to research.

   But: ....

Work out which noun should be changed to a verb. Then rewrite:

6 **Not:** We achieved purification of the atmosphere.

   But: ....

7 **Not:** We brought the experiment to a successful conclusion.

   But: ....

8 **Not:** The staff must make adjustments to the new timetable.

   But: ....

9 **Not:** The prime minister will present a report on the state of the economy.

   But: ....

10 **Not:** I shall take into consideration your recommendations.

   But: ....

You Can Write

Answers:
1 The device measured (verb) the surface area.
2 A colour code identifies (verb) the substance.
3 Muscular strength increased (verb) because of exercise.
or
Exercise increased (verb) muscular strength.
4 The article summarises (verb) the problem
5 The grant stimulated (verb) research.
6 We purified (verb) the atmosphere.
7 We successfully concluded (verb) the experiment.
8 The staff must adjust (verb) to the new timetable.
9 The prime minister will report (verb) on the state of the economy.
10 I shall consider (verb) your recommendations.

List the five basic principles of effective writing. Then check your answers.

1 ....
2 ....
3 ....
4 ....
5 ....

Now for some practice:
Rewrite the following in the spaces provided. You can reorganise them in any way you like, provided you don't alter the meaning. See how many words you can save. Remember that brevity is pointless if you omit essential information.

1 There are three conclusions that can be drawn from the results.

  ....

2 In private schools, it is expected that boys will keep their hair short.

  ....

  ....

3 It is probable the fish will return to the river once antipollution measures are adopted by the state government.

  ....

  ....

28

Developing an Effective Style

4 He spoke in a hesitant manner.

5 Pot is smoked by so many students that the laws are not enforced by the school authorities.

6 She is the girl who is wearing the yellow coat.

7 He lives in the neighbourhood of the football oval.

8 They spoke in regard to politics.

9 The solution is to rewrite the sentence in different words.

10 The money was a great encouragement to the team.

11 There are many Australians who drink in a heavy manner.

12 His corpulent body contains excess adipose tissue.

13 The noise level was highest in the immediate vicinity of the machine.

14 The company had a complaint from a customer to the effect that, on consuming the hamburger, nausea of the stomach had been experienced.

15 The performance of the duties were carried out successfully.

16 Analysis was carried out on the chemical.

You Can Write

17 The reason for this increase in spending was probably due to poor bookkeeping.

....

18 A reduction in costs was able to be achieved.

....

19 Within a short period of time the experiment will reach a state of conclusion.

....

20 The author of this report is cognisant of the details.

....

Some possibilities. You may have done better.
1 Three conclusions can be drawn from the results.
2 Private schools expect boys to keep their hair short.
3 Fish will probably return to the river once the state government adopts antipollution measures.
4 He spoke hesitantly.
5 So many students smoke pot that school authorities ignore (or don't enforce) the law.
6 She is the girl in the yellow coat.
7 He lives near the football oval.
8 They spoke about politics.
9 The solution is to rewrite the sentence.
10 The money greatly encouraged the team.
11 Many Australians drink heavily.
12 He is fat.
13 The noise level was highest near the machine.
   or
   It was noisiest near the machine.
14 A customer complained that the hamburger made him feel ill.
15 The duties were performed successfully.
16 The chemical was analysed.
   (Possible: I analysed the chemical).
17 Spending probably increased because of poor bookkeeping.
18 Costs were reduced.
   or
   We reduced costs.
19 The experiment will end soon.
20 The author knows the details.
   or
   I know the details.

This chapter has given you a few suggestions on how to develop a more effective style. The best way to develop a

Developing an Effective Style

good style is by practice. Even quite experienced authors must continually check their expression. For example, I originally wrote in an earlier draft of this manual, 'the following hints may help you prune the number of words you use'. The editor suggested 'the following hints may help you prune the excess', thus replacing five words with one. Don't spend hours worrying over single sentences or paragraphs. Just be aware of the principles and aim to develop a clear, concise style.

3 Planning your Essay

In almost every course you take, whether at school or at a tertiary institution, you will be required to write an essay at some stage. Essays serve a number of functions, including:

- Helping you to clarify your ideas. The process of writing an essay forces you to organise your thoughts, to realise what you don't know about a topic, and to present a coherent, logical argument or analysis.
- Giving you practice in developing an effective writing style that will be useful when you enter the workforce. The skills needed to write a report, business letter or manual are essentially the same as those required for an essay.
- Helping examiners to assess students. Some subjects are assessed entirely through essay questions.

The ability to write a good essay, therefore, is very important. You need to develop a **system** to make your essay writing easier and more effective.

Steps in planning your essay

Step one: analyse the essay topic

Most students ignore this step, yet it is vital.
 You must know exactly what you are required to do; otherwise you can't prepare or write. You must answer the specific question, not what you *think* the question is. Look carefully for the words that tell you what to do. A full list of these words and their meanings is on the next page.

Planning your Essay

Analyse . . . . to break something down so as to find the main ideas, and then show how they are related and why they are important.
Comment on . . . . to discuss, criticise or explain its meaning.
Compare . . . . to show both the similarities and differences.
Contrast . . . . to compare by showing the differences.
Criticise . . . . to give your judgement or reasoned opinion of something, showing its good and bad points.
Define . . . . to give the exact meaning.
Discuss . . . . to examine, giving the details and the points for and against. You must develop a logical argument backed by sound evidence.
Enumerate . . . . to list, name and number the main ideas one by one.
Evaluate . . . . to give your judgement, after showing the advantages and disadvantages.
Illustrate . . . . to explain or make it clear by concrete examples. Sometimes you may use a figure or a diagram.
Interpret . . . . to give the meaning. You give your own opinions, backed by evidence.
Justify . . . . to show why you think it is right. Give reasons for your statement or conclusion.
List . . . . (same as enumerate.)
Outline . . . . to give a general summary of the main ideas, supported by secondary ideas. Omit minor details.
Prove . . . . to show by argument or logic that it is true. You must provide adequate evidence.
Relate . . . . to show the connections.
Review . . . . to make a survey in which you look critically at the important parts.
State . . . . to specify the main points in precise terms. Omit minor details.
Summarise . . . . to give a concise account of the main ideas. Omit details and examples.
Trace . . . . to follow the progress or history of a topic.

You Can Write

A. Describe *(outline, state, summarise, define, enumerate, list, trace, illustrate)*

This sort of essay topic is usually a straightforward exercise in finding the main ideas, writing them down in a logical, chronological or spatial order in your own words and giving examples where necessary. You may be asked to do this in detail or to provide a summary.

For example:
- Describe some of the problems associated with anthropological field work.
- Summarise the events leading up to the French Revolution.
- Describe the photosynthesis process in plants.
- List the types of bonding that may occur between atoms.

You are not asked to be critical. You are asked to set down the facts. You should, however, let the reader know from where you have obtained your information. It is important, therefore, that you reference fully. (Chapter 9 deals with this topic.)

B. Analyse *(criticise, discuss, evaluate, interpret, justify, prove, argue)*

This sort of essay topic asks you to do more. While you still need to find and describe the main facts and ideas, you also need to be critical. You will give reasons for or against a point of view, criticise (examine the positive and negative aspects), compare and contrast. At undergraduate level, especially at first year, you will not usually be expected to come up with many original ideas, but you will need to show that you have read different points of view and used the evidence you have collected from the authorities on the subject to develop an argument. Thorough, accurate referencing is, therefore, vital. In some subjects you can express your own view drawn from your own experiences, but you can't rely on your own experiences alone; you must demonstrate that you are aware of and understand other viewpoints, even if you don't necessarily agree with them. And if you don't agree with them, you must be able to demolish the argument with convincing logic or facts.

Planning your Essay

For example:

> To what extent were white Australians racist in the nineteenth century?

You may conclude that they were or they were not, or they were to some extent. Your analysis will consist of discussing various historians' interpretations and, from these, arriving at some conclusion. In tackling this question, you might start with a general history of the period, perhaps your textbook. Note the main facts and opinions. You may find that the author summarises various arguments; if so, note them carefully. Use the bibliography or list of references so that you can refer directly to the sources the author used.
Another example:

> Evaluate the contribution of Darwin's theory of evolution to the development of science in the nineteenth century.

You may find that scholars disagree as to the importance of the theory. You will need to examine the various arguments as critically as you can and then come to some conclusion. Follow the general principles as set out for the previous question. Make sure that you answer the question: note that this question is about Darwin's theory of evolution, not about the life of Darwin. If you don't analyse the essay topic carefully, you may easily misinterpret it.

Often a question will consist of a quotation, usually a controversial statement or proposition. You will then be asked to discuss this.

> 'A person's relative share of any social resource results not from 'natural' inequalities but from socially produced ones.' Discuss this statement, concentrating on any two social resources.

In this type of question, you need to be very careful that you understand exactly what the quotation means. Try to locate the book or article that contains the quotation, as reading it in context may help you understand it better, that is, of course, if the lecturer has not made up the topic. If in doubt, ask the lecturer or tutor.

Also, in this type of question, you will often find words or phrases (groups of words) that are very specific to the subject.
For example:

> social resource
> 'natural' inequalities
> socially produced inequalities

You *must* clearly understand what these mean before you can competently answer the question. Your textbooks may help you. Often far more useful, however, are the many specialised dictionaries and encyclopedias, which are available for all subjects.
For example:

> *A Dictionary of Physical Sciences*
> *The Encyclopedia of the Social Sciences*

(Note: The definitions in general dictionaries, such as the *Collins English Dictionary*, are too broad and general for your purposes.) The librarian at your library's information desk can show you where to find these specialised dictionaries and encyclopedias. You can also find them yourself by looking in the library's subject catalogue under the subject heading.
For example:

> Physics — Dictionaries and Encylopedias

Planning your Essay

C. Describe and analyse

Some questions will ask you to both describe and analyse. *For example*:

> Outline Darwin's theory of evolution. Evaluate its contribution to the development of science in the nineteenth century.

The first part is simply a summary of the theory, while the second asks you critically to evaluate its impact.

Step two: survey the literature

This step is very important, but often ignored. It means simply seeing what material is available and then sorting it out into different groups: What is the best introduction? What should I read next? What should be left until later?

Many students simply pick up the first book at hand and start furiously taking notes. Then they grab another and go through the same process. They read and they take notes without any real aim, purpose or system. This is inefficient, depressing, and disheartening.

Unselective reading and notetaking for essays are probably the greatest wasters of students' time.

How, then, do you select suitable references?

- Your lecturer or tutor may make suggestions. However, some students assume that what is suggested is the only material worth reading. This is very seldom the case. Also, if many students are taking the course, you will find that the recommended materials will very quickly disappear. In most cases, however, you will be able to find material that is just as useful — if not more useful — than what your lecturer suggests. This is especially so in the humanities and social sciences.
- Essay, tutorial or course reading lists will also be useful. The materials on these, however, will be greatly in demand and perhaps impossible to locate. Sometimes these lists are inaccurate or out-of-date.

37

- Other students or library staff can help. But this is a very hit-and-miss way of finding materials.

It is essential, if you have not done so already, to learn to use the library.

- You will waste hours browsing aimlessly among the shelves if you don't. The knowledge explosion is rapidly increasing the size of library holdings. You can't rely on a hit-and-miss method.
- You need to become an independent student who does not have to rely on being spoon-fed by the lecturer or tutor.
- You need to develop your research skills at some stage. Why not start immediately?

Most libraries conduct group or individual tours. If you have not yet been on one, do so as soon as possible. Each library has its own character. The section at the end of this chapter on **how to locate books and journal articles** is a general introduction to help you make the best use of the library.

Step three: get a rough, general overview before you start taking detailed notes

Skim-read an introductory reference or references. Get an idea of the issues and questions that arise from your reading. Think about these. Note key words and ideas. Get the main facts. Note any disagreements of interpretation. **Get the overall picture.**

Step four: now take notes effectively

Start with a short, easy, general introduction if you can. You don't want to waste your time or confuse yourself, so do not take the same points down more than once. A surprising number of students rush in and start notetaking without thinking first what they are doing. They either copy out vast chunks of useless information, or they keep copying the same information from different sources. Before

Planning your Essay

you take down any notes from a book or journal article, ask yourself: 'What do I want to get from this — the major point, some statistics, a particular point of view, or what?' **Read for a specific purpose.**

Don't try to write an essay directly from books open in front of you. Unless you are highly skilled, you will plagiarise; that is, use somebody else's words as your own. (See chapter 9)

You can save much time and effort by photocopying key articles or chapters of books. However, don't waste your time and money by copying everything. Some articles, for example, may contain only a few pages or even sentences of relevant material, and it may be quicker and much cheaper to take notes,. If you do photocopy, write the publication details on the first page.

To save time and energy, use the BFAR, or a similar, reading method:

B = Browse
Quickly glance through the reference. Glance at the contents page, index, headings, illustrations, the bold (**heavy**) type, diagrams, summaries and any other aids that the author provides. Get a feel for the reference. Get the overall picture.

F = Focus
Skim-read again. Concentrate on the introduction and conclusion, if any. Ask yourself: 'What are the main points?' The first paragraph of each chapter usually tells you what it's about.

A = Absorb
By now you should know what you are looking for. You should have some idea of the **overall picture**. Start to underline the **main** points. (Not in a library book or journal.) Use highlight pens. Take accurate, concise notes (see below).

The last step — **reinforce** — may not be necessary when you are taking notes for an essay.

R = Reinforce
You must do this if you want to remember what you have noted down. Most students neglect this step. This is a pity because, although it should not take much extra time, it will greatly improve your ability to recall what you have read. This step is vital if you are dealing with factual material that must be memorised. One way of reinforcing is to write a summary in your own words. To help fix it in your long-term memory, you should read it aloud.

The reinforcing step is very important when you are reading for an examination.

Notetaking

Before you start taking notes, ask yourself what use you are going to make of this particular reference. You will get different points from each reference you use. An early reference may give you a series of main points, but in a later reference you may only be interested in a single piece of evidence.

Write on one side of the paper only, as this will make it much easier to organise your notes. We'll discuss this later.

Leave plenty of space.

Each time you start a new book, head your notes with the author, title, place of publication, publisher and date of publication. For journal articles, write down the author, title of article, title of journal, volume number, issue number, date of publication and page numbers of article.

You must identify *each* page of notes very clearly with: the author, title and page number.

As you take notes, write the number of the page you are reading and note it in the margin of your notes.

Use quotation marks if you copy material directly.

You must stop taking notes at some stage. You can't read everything that has been written on the topic. Don't forget that you will be marked on what you write, not on how many notes you have collected. You can even leave some of your notetaking until after you have written a draft, when you'll

Planning your Essay

know exactly what you want. It probably will make your notetaking much more effective.

Time allocation

Most inexperienced students do not allow enough time for the actual writing of the essay. This is partly because they, like some more experienced authors, find it easier to take notes than to face up to the more difficult writing task. Remember that you will be judged and marked on what you have written, not on the volume of notes you have made.

A rough guide to time allocation:

> 60% analysis of the topic and collection of information
> 40% organising and sorting of information, writing, rewriting, polishing.

Organising your notes

- You've collected a pile of notes.
- You decide to start writing.
- You organise your desk, sharpen your pencils, place your writing paper on the desk.
- Now what do you do?

At this stage, without some system, many students either waste a great deal of time or even give up. They read through their notes a few times, and become increasingly confused and discouraged. They may decide to gather more notes, or wander away for a while, or reorganise their desks. Eventually they may pick up a pencil and start thinking of something to write about.

But what if that uncompromising sheet of blank paper still doesn't offer any help?

As with any writing, you need some system, especially to get started. Chapters 2 and 3 will help you.

Your main task is to organise your mass of notes into units that correspond to the major sections into which you will divide the essay.

You Can Write

Consider adopting the following suggestions to help you organise your notes:

Some experts strongly recommend that you **'brainstorm'**:

- Read through your notes a few times.
- Take a blank sheet of paper.
- Jot down roughly and quickly what you consider to be the major points.
- Now reorganise them so that one leads on logically and naturally to the next.
- Separate the major from the minor points.

Then, decide what you think will be the major sections within the essay. You will probably find that your essay will naturally divide into about five to seven main sections, including an introduction and a conclusion. Each of these sections will deal with one main point in the essay. Each section will consist of one or, more likely, a number of paragraphs.

By brainstorming you will get something down on paper quickly. It will give your mind something to work upon. You will have broken the essay down into more manageable units. It's now beginning to take shape.

Let's say you are writing an essay on Freud's influence on psychology. Your major sections might work out as:

	Introduction
A	Freud's background
B	Psychology before Freud
C	Freud's theory: his early writings
D	Freud's theory: his later writings
E	His followers: the development of his theory
F	His critics
	Conclusion

Now that you have decided upon the major sections, you can use one of a number of systems to organise the notes. Find the one that suits you best. But you must develop some system. I've suggested three.

Planning your Essay

(In case you make a mess of things, you might photocopy your notes before organising the first few essays.)

System A

Collect all your notes. Decide on some system of coding, that is, some way of organising your pages of notes in some order.

For example:
> You can use the letters of each section A, B, C, etc. in the margin. Alternatively you can use colours: Yellow = Section A; Blue = Section B, etc.

Code your notes with letters or colours to show which sections they belong to. For example: Yellow = Freud's Background. Blue = Psychology theory before Freud.

When you have finished, summarise your notes again on a separate sheet of paper under each section heading.

Note: **If you summarise your notes, you will be less likely to plagiarise (use another person's words) accidentally.**
(See Chapter 9 for a discussion of plagiarism.)

Now you can start writing.

System B ('Scissors and Paste')

Lay out all your notes.
Code them (as above).
Cut them up and rearrange under the appropriate headings, each on a separate sheet of paper. (You can tape them on very large sheets of paper if you wish.)
Start writing.
The main advantage of System B is that it is very quick. The disadvantage is that you can easily mix up your notes and lose them.

Planning your Essay

System C

Some students write their notes on cards, using a new card for each major point. However, you will probably end up with a huge number of cards. This system is best suited to a major thesis, but you might adopt it. I do not recommend this system to undergraduate students.

When you've organised your notes, you can start drawing up an **outline**, that is the listing of major and minor points under each main section of the essay.

How to find books and journal articles

Finding books

The **general catalogue** will list all the books held in the library. A particular book may be located by **author or title or subject**. Note how the book *Venomous Creatures of Australia: A Field Guide with Notes on First Aid*, by Struan K. Sutherland is listed under the three headings. The unique number assigned to that book is on the upper left corner. Use it to find the book on the shelves.

You Can Write

Author (Use this list to locate books when you know the author's name.)
For example:

> 615.942   SUTHERLAND Struan K[eith]
> Australian animal toxins: the creatures, their toxins, and care of the poisoned patient/Struan K Sutherland – – Melbourne: Oxford University Press 1968 – – 527p.

> 591.6903   SUTHERLAND, Struan K[eith]
> Venomous creatures of Australia: a field guide with notes on first aid/Struan K Sutherland – – Melbourne: Oxford University Press, 1981 – 128p.

> 615.1   SUTHERLAND, Violette Cutter
> A synopsis of pharmacology – – 2nd ed. – – Philadelphia: Sanders, 1970 – 720p.

Title (Use this list to locate books when you know the title.)
For example:

> 591.69
> Venomous Australian animals dangerous to man / edited by J. Ros. Garner– –3rd ed.– –Parkville, Vic.: Commonwealth Serum Laboratories, 1972– –86p.

> 591.6903
> Venomous creatures of Australia: a field guide with notes on first aid Struan K. Sutherland– –Melbourne: Oxford University Press, 1981– –128p.

> 616.135
> Venous and arterial thrombosis, evaluation, prevention, and management / W. R. Pitney – – Edinburgh : Churchill Livingstone, 1981 – 231p.

Planning your Essay

Subject (Use this list to find books on a particular topic. Under each subject heading you will find a list of books relating to that subject, such as 'Poisonous Animals'.)
For example:

> POISONOUS ANIMALS — AUSTRALIA
> 615.942
> Australian animal toxins: the creatures, their toxins, and care of the poisoned patient/Struan K. Sutherland — — Melbourne : Oxford University Press, 1982 — — 572p.

> 591.6903　　POISONOUS ANIMALS — AUSTRALIA
> Venomous creatures of Australia : a field guide with notes on first aid / Struan K. Sutherland — — Melbourne : Oxford University Press, 1981 — — 128p.

> POISONOUS ANIMALS — AUSTRALIA
> 591.69
> Venomous Australian animals dangerous to man / edited by J. Ros. Garner — — 3rd ed. — — Parkville, Vic. : Commonwealth Serum Laboratories, 1972 — — 86p.

Note: When you find one book on your subject, look at the bottom of catalogue card, where you will find one or two subject headings given for that book. Other books on the same subject will have cards under those headings in the catalogue.

From the catalogue you can usually find:
- where the book is located — 591.6903 plus some letters; (libraries use different systems)
- the author's full name — Struan Keith Sutherland
- the book's full title — *Venomous Creatures of Australia: A Field Guide with Notes on First Aid.*

Other useful information that may be included is:
- the place of publication — Melbourne
- the publisher — Oxford University Press

47

You Can Write

- the date of publication — 1982
- number of pages — 128
- the edition — (if more than one)

Whether it has illustrations, maps, bibliography and index

The library will also contain **bibliographies** (list of books) of books in print, such as the *British National Bibliography*. With these, you can find the titles of books that are not held in the library you are using. You can borrow these books by making an interlibrary loan request at your library.

Finding journal articles

Journals are publications that usually come out at regular intervals. Each issue of a journal prints a number of articles by different authors. Journal articles can be very useful because the most recent ones are more up-to-date in their information, news and research than are books. Because they usually cover only one topic, you do not have to sift through masses of information you do not want. Journal articles are not listed separately in the library's catalogue, although the titles of the journals are. The task of locating a journal article on a particular topic would be enormous if there were not very handy aids available:

Journal catalogue

> Most libraries have a list (catalogue) of the journals held in that particular library. This only tells you what journals are available in the library and where they can be found. This catalogue does not help you find specific articles.

Indexing journals

> These are special journals that regularly list (index) the articles published in a range of journals within a certain subject field. For example, the *Australian Education Index* indexes the contents of dozens of Australian education journals. Indexing journals usually come out monthly or quarterly and then are commulated in one volume at the end of each year. If you are looking for a journal article, it may

Planning your Essay

save time to start with the latest commulated volume. An indexing journal has a series of subject headings arranged in alphabetical order. Under each subject heading is a list of articles on that subject and the details of the journals in which they were printed, including page numbers.

Abstracting journals

These are special kinds of indexing journals. Not only do they provide the same information, but they also contain a brief summary (abstract) of every article they list. For example, *Psychology Abstracts* gives summaries of hundreds of articles in psychology journals every month.

These aids are there to help students. Your library will have indexing and abstracting journals to cover all of the teaching subjects. Ask a librarian to help you find the best one for your topic. You can order particular articles through interlibrary loan, too. Once you learn how to find journal articles, you will soon appreciate that they are often the most useful resource in your library.

4 Organising your Essay

An essay consists of:

- **an introduction**
- **a body**
- **a conclusion.**

The introduction to the essay

Remember that the key to successful writing is: **getting started — getting something down on paper fast**. Very often you are not certain what the essay is really about, and so you can't write a polished introduction until you have written at least the first draft of the essay. On the other hand, some students like to write a good introduction before they progress any further. The choice is yours. However, if you are not careful, you may waste hours on your introduction. As a general rule, I suggest that you **write the introduction very quickly and roughly. Polish it up later. You may even leave the introduction until last**.

The introduction can be written in different ways, depending upon the topic. Your **introduction** will perform some of the following functions:

- Give the reader an idea what the essay is about.
- Say what sort of essay it is (e.g. describes, explains).
- Outline the approach or the argument.
- Relate the problem briefly to other studies.
- Tell the reader what the thesis (topic, theme) statement is. What is the main idea or argument? Not every essay will have a thesis statement (e.g. essays that ask you to describe rather than analyse).
- Interest the reader. The introduction should encourage the reader to read on.

Organising your Essay

The following is typical of a first-year undergraduate essay:

> This essay is about the psychoanalyist Sigmund Freud. It will discuss his psychoanalytic theory. The essay will describe Freud's theory of the development of personality and its contribution to psychology and psychiatry. Finally, the essay will discuss some of the major criticisms of the theory.

This would be an excellent first draft introduction. It sets out very clearly what the writer is going to do. After the writer has finished the whole first draft, he might revise the introduction to read:

> Sigmund Freud, a Viennese neurologist who lived from 1856 to 1939, was the father of psychoanalysis. His theory attempts to explain how personality develops in people. Freud's psychoanalytic theory has greatly influenced the development of psychology and psychiatry, but many critics have rejected it.

You've said virtually the same thing, but in a different way. Notice that the last sentence is the proposition or thesis statement that you'll be discussing.

Keep your introductions short. Do not provide details. You want to make a general statement, that is, to let the reader know quickly what the essay is about.
For example:

> D.H. Lawrence's most famous novel, *Sons and Lovers*, is intensely autobiographical. Many of the characters and incidents in the novel relate almost directly to Lawrence's own life experiences and to those of his family and acquaintances.

Note what happens when you insert irrelevant detail in the introduction to the essay on Freud:

> Sigmund Freud, a Viennese neurologist who lived from 1856 to 1939, was the father of psychoanalysis. When he was three years old, his parents took him to Leipzig, but he returned to Vienna. His theory attempts to explain how personality develops in people. Freud's first published work, *On Aphasia*, was a study of the neurological disorder in which the ability to pronounce words is lost as a result of brain damage. He

collaborated with the Viennese physician Josef Breuer on a study of hysteria. Freud's psychoanalytic theory has greatly influenced the development of psychology and psychiatry, but many critics have rejected it.

This introduction is now too long. The specific details about his early life and about his work do not belong in the introduction: they could instead be discussed within the body of the essay.

Now consider the following introduction. Note how it opens with a very general comment about Indian influence on southeast Asia and then becomes more specific. However, it is too long and contains specific details that should be omitted.

Underline the thesis statement, that is the argument that the body of the essay must support, and cross out the irrelevant sections:

> One of the major themes of Eurasian history is the impact of India upon the development of civilisations in archipelago southeast Asia. The very name 'Indonesia' itself suggests that the archipelago was strongly influenced by India. Throughout Indonesia, there is abundant direct evidence of Indian examples, particularly in literature, religious symbolism, art and archaeological remains. It would be easy, therefore, to assume, as have many scholars, that Indonesian civilisation is a weak shadow of a culturally dominant neighbour.
> Borobudur in Java, for example, is very similar to Buddhist stupas found in India: it is truly one of the world's greatest religious monuments. In fact, although India provided some inspiration at the early stage of development, indigenous efforts and talents eventually created a distinctive civilisation in which Indian elements were vastly modified.

The thesis statement is contained in the last sentence beginning 'In fact . . . '

Your introduction should be concise. A single paragraph of about five sentences is usually long enough. Note how the example above could be condensed:

> A major theme of Eurasian history is the impact of India upon the development of civilisations in archipelago southeast

Asia. The very name 'Indonesia' suggests that the archipelago was strongly influenced by India. Throughout Indonesia, there is abundant direct evidence of Indian examples, and it would be easy to assume, as have many scholars, that Indonesia is a weak shadow of a culturally dominant neighbour. In fact, although India provided some inspiration at the early stages of development, indigenous efforts and talents eventually created a distinctive civilisation in which Indian elements were vastly modified.

Keep the introduction very general. Don't provide detailed, specific information. You do not normally need to reference the introduction. Remember it is an **introduction** — your aim is to allow your reader to meet the topic.

- Don't answer the question in the introduction. If you do, the reader will have no interest in reading further.
- Don't apologise in your introduction ('This essay is an inadequate . . . '). If you do, it will be held against you!
- Don't make rash promises in your introduction. If you state that you are going to do something, make sure that you do.

The body of the essay

Get the rest of the essay on paper fast.

The body of the essay consists of **paragraphs**, each dealing with **one** aspect of the essay. (We shall discuss paragraphing in the next chapter.)

Each major section of the essay will consist of one or more related paragraphs. Take the essay on Freud that I've mentioned before. You could organise it like this:

Section A. Freud's background
One paragraph

Section B. Psychology theory before Freud
Four paragraphs:

>Psychology in the classical world
>Christian views of the psychology of man
>The theories of John Brown
>The Berlin School

What you've done is broken down what seems to be a huge, indigestible essay into smaller, more manageable units. If you organise like this, you will never have to face the major problem that confronts inexperienced writers: **How do I find enough words**? Proper organisation will solve this particular problem immediately.

Instead of writing a draft of the entire essay, you might write each section at a time. The principle is to write as much as you can at each writing session and to start writing immediately you have finished your preparation. (See chapter 1.)

The conclusion to the essay

The conclusion — the final paragraph(s) — should leave the reader with the feeling that the essay is finished, not that the writer has just given up!

- It should generally answer the sorts of questions raised in the introduction.
- You may stress one major point or summarise several points.
- Don't introduce new material. You may occasionally, however, point out further questions that have arisen but which would require another essay to answer.
- The conclusion should be a general statement. Don't go into details.
- If possible, make your final sentence the strongest. Finish strongly.
- Keep your conclusion short.
- Consider the following examples taken from students' essays.

Example A. A Psychology Essay:

> Regardless of whether one accepts or rejects all or part of Freud's theory, its impact has been enormous. No other original thinker in psychology has had such a wide effect on psychological debate and research. The debate about the value of the theory makes up a large volume of literature. Despite this, many aspects of Freud's theory still remain an enigma.

(Now reread the introduction to this essay.)

Example B. A Literature Essay:

> *Sons and Lovers* is one of Lawrence's most brilliant novels because it is so intensely personal. Many incidents and emotions, especially in the first half of the novel, almost mirrored those in Lawrence's life. But perhaps it is the complex sexual relations of the main characters in the novel that most strongly and vividly echo the frustrations, guilt and unhappiness of Lawrence's young manhood,

(Note how this restates the earlier introduction but also provides a general summary.)

Example C. A History Essay:

> Indian civilisation exerted a considerable influence on Indonesia, but the evidence suggests that it was gradually assimilated and adapted rather than blindly copied. Visual data — such as temple architecture, Batik designs, shadow plays — can be traced to Indian sources, but they also bear witness to the Indonesians' ability to merge their indigenous beliefs and ideas with those of India. No doubt we would find different cultures existing in Indonesia if it had not been for the introduction of Indian civilisation. In time, however, what was originally Indian became transmuted and synthesised into a civilisation that was uniquely Indonesian.

(A longer summary. Note the very strong concluding sentence. Now go back and read the introduction to this particular essay. Note how this conclusion restates the thesis in a stronger fashion.)

A good, clear, interesting introduction and conclusion will greatly strengthen your essay. First and last impressions are very important.

Presenting your Essay

- Careful presentation will improve your mark. Lecturers find it very difficult to take sloppily presented work seriously. Leave time at the end for final corrections and general tidying up.

You Can Write

- Attend to the minor details. Be as precise as possible. Be consistent in setting out. It really takes very little extra time to do things properly, such as having the same width of margins throughout, and underlining titles of books and journals. For a little more effort, you can gain a great deal.
- Type your essay if possible, although good handwriting is better than poor typing. Research, however, has shown that well-typed essays score higher than those that are handwritten. Typing also helps you to spot weaknesses and errors. If you can't type, either learn or pay some good typist to do it for you. 'Two-finger' typing with lots of corrections is a poor use of time and a waste of energy.
- Leave a wide margin (40 mm) at the left-hand side of your paper for comments by the lecturer.

Presenting Reports

Science and commerce departments sometimes require students to prepare reports. The chief difference between report and essay writing is in the method of presentation of the material. The same principles of good writing — clarity, brevity and simplicity — apply to both. But reports are organised so that the reader can select and skim the material, rather than read every section.

- Present the information in declining order of importance:
  Subject
     Summary of Findings
        Body of Report
           Detailed Information (surveys, statistics, etc.)
- In the body of the report, present the information in hierarchical order, using spacing and numbered headings to guide the reader. Breaking the topic into units and highlighting the key points makes your work easier both to write and read. Set your headings out very clearly. Use capital letters and underlining. Cramped work is confusing and irritating, so use plenty of space.

For example:

6 <u>EMPLOYMENT PROSPECTS</u>

While recruitment to the public service has declined over the last five years, we expect that this trend will be reversed next year.

6.1 TEACHING

Teachers still constitute a large proportion of government employees. This will continue, although there will be a decline in the primary sector.

6.1.1 <u>Primary Teaching</u>

The decline in the numbers of primary teachers is a reflection of the fall in the birthrate.

You Can Write

Note the use of different kinds of headings and of numbers. Note also the generous spacing between headings.

- If necessary, use tables, diagrams, graphs, illustrations, flow charts (see next section). These may be the most effective way of providing information. If they will help the reader, use them; if not, don't.
- Summarise your findings in the body of the report. Put all the details in one or more appendixes (e.g. copies of questionnaires, complete survey results, statistical data, references).
- However good the material in a report, it cannot survive sloppy presentation. Pay attention to the small details, which ensure that you turn in a professional job. Use correct, clear English. Proofread your work; don't blame the typist for errors. Take pride in your ability to write well.

Tables and figures

Tables and figures (graphs, charts, diagrams, maps) can help you communicate more effectively. They are generally used to convey detailed or complex statistical data, or to show the interrelationships of a number of parts. Use them only when necessary. Ask yourself:

- What is the function of this table or figure?
- Is this the best way to convey the information?

Don't use tables or figures simply for effect. It would be pointless and distracting to draw up a table to demonstrate that Political Party A won 56% of the seats in an election while Party B won 46%.

Tables should be placed either:

- In the text (often on a separate page) if they are essential to the argument or conclusions. These tables usually are relatively simple and uncomplicated. Place them as close as possible to where they are first mentioned.

or

- At the end of the essay or report (in an appendix) if they contain detailed statistical data that would distract the

Organising your Essay

reader if placed in the body of the essay or report. You may produce a simplified summary of an appendix and include this in the text.

- Number each table consecutively.
- Set out the title clearly beneath the table.
- Take plenty of room when setting out.
- Rule up according to the nature of the data you want to present.

Table 1.1   Area of the States and Mainland Territories of Australia

States and Mainland Territories	Area (sq. km)
Western Australia	2,527,621
Queensland	1,727,522
Northern Territory	1,347,519
South Australia	984,377
New South Wales	801,428
Victoria	227,619
Tasmania	68,332
Australian Capital Territory	2,432
Total	7,686,849

Graphs and charts are often a better way of presenting numerical data than tables.

Graphs

Clearly label them.

Fig. 9.1   Population change in country A, 1910–1950

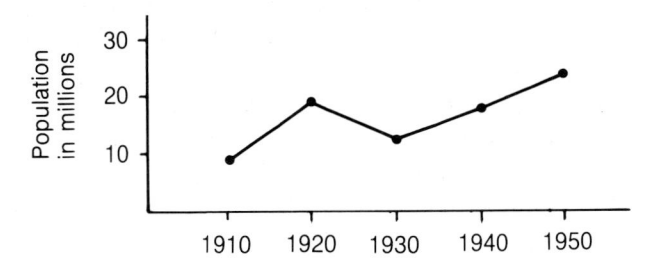

You Can Write

Bar graphs

Fig. 7.1   Mortality rate per 100,000 persons, 1910–1950

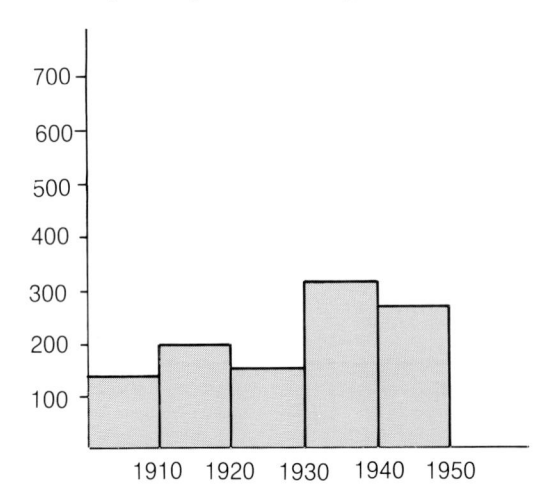

Bar graph showing comparison.

Fig. 2.1   Electricity costs in households A and B (January–April 1984)

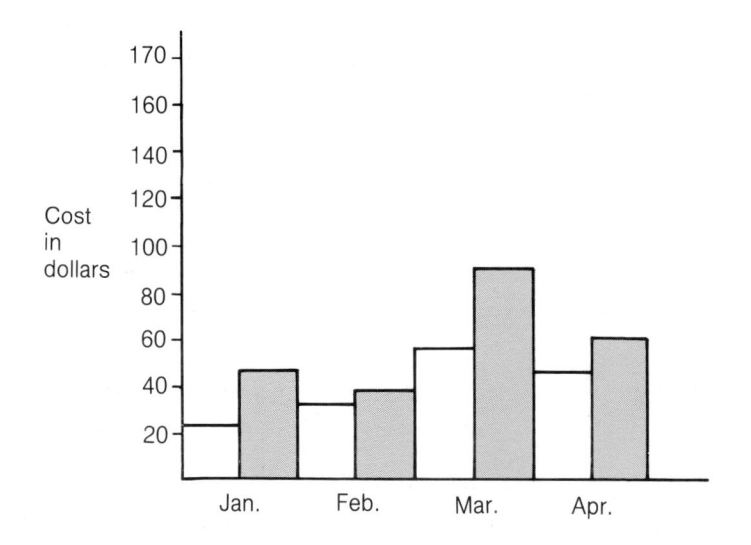

Organising your Essay

Pie chart
Useful for showing proportions and percentages.

Fig. 6.1   Birthplace of migrants in town B

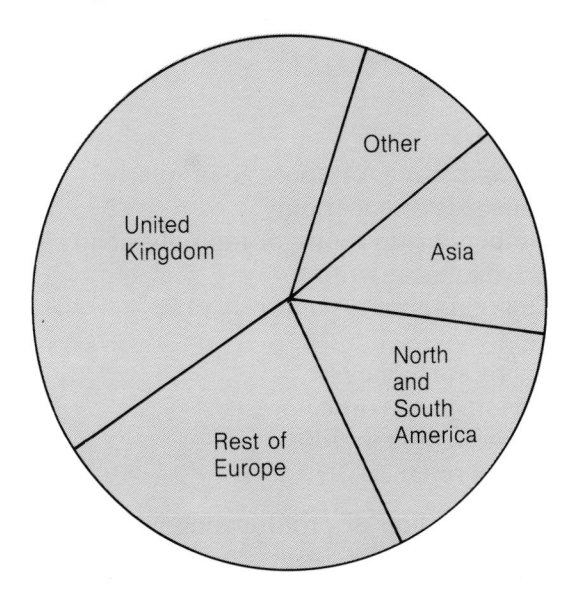

You can use many other kinds of diagrams, charts and illustrations, such as flow charts, to help you communicate better. As with other forms of communication, keep them as simple and as uncluttered as you can.

- Write or type on one side of the page only.
- Use one-and-a-half or double line spacing.
- Number the pages in the top centre or top right-hand corner.
- Proofread your work carefully. You must accept responsibility for what you submit. Blaming the typist will not work.

One final point. Being human beings, lecturers will be very impressed by an essay that is neatly presented, carefully typed, and thoroughly and consistently referenced. The slight extra effort of attending to relatively minor details will be well rewarded. It will not by itself guarantee you a good

mark, but it most certainly will improve your chances. It will also give you a sense of pride and achievement.

The Essay Check List may help you make sure that you have attended to all the details.

Essay check list

1 Presentation:

- standard paper size (A4, foolscap or quarto)
- type on one side of paper only
- pages numbered (top centre or top right-hand corner)
- accurate typing/neat writing
- straight margin (about 40 mm)
- proofread by yourself
- proofread by someone else*
- staple top left-hand corner
- title of essay written in *full*
- copy of essay retained

* An excellent method of proofreading is to read your copy to somebody else, who corrects his/her copy of your work.

2 Essay structure and organisation:

Introduction

- concise
- interesting
- outlines the problem
- provides a thesis statement (not always possible)

Paragraphs

- not too long
- not too short
- each deals with one aspect of essay
- all sentences within each paragraph are related
- paragraphs linked together
- paragraphs in logical order
- serve some purpose/help answer the question

Conclusion

- ties everything together
- summarises argument (briefly)
- is effective

3 Argument:

- all aspects of topic covered
- essay balanced (each aspect adequately discussed)
- definitions (where required)
- argument developed logically
- argument convincing/makes sense to somebody else (spouse, friend, etc.)
- generalisations supported with specific examples (evidence)
- draws on a number of sources

4 Plagiarism, direct quotations, references:

Quotations

- for specific purpose (functional)
- used infrequently
- generally short
- set out correctly

References

- all direct quotations, maps, tables, diagrams
- all facts, theories, opinions not your own
- clear distinction between references and your statements/interpretations
- reference list (or bibliography) set out correctly

5 Style:

- no headings in formal essays
- flows (reads easily)
- concise
- clear
- unpretentious
- no abbreviations, (e.g., etc., i.e.)

6 Spelling and grammar:

- correctly spelled (N.B. importance of proofreading)
- consistent use of capitalisation
- correct grammar

5 Paragraphing

The aim of paragraphing is to help your reader. By dividing the whole essay up into units, each of which deals with one, and only one, idea, you can guide your reader along. Your ideas or arguments become easier to follow, as the reader is given a short break between each step. When paragraphing, therefore, keep in mind that you are doing it for your and your reader's sakes, not to make the essay look right: paragraphing serves a very definitive function and has a very important role in effective essay or report writing.

- **The paragraph is the building block of your essay.**
- **Each paragraph deals with one aspect of the topic.**
- **Each paragraph is a unit.** It has a topic sentence (usually the first) that tells what the paragraph is about, a middle containing the sentences that explain, illustrate or develop what is in the topic sentence, and a concluding sentence.
- **The topic sentence controls the material in the other sentences in the paragraph.**

The sentences that follow the topic sentence should relate to the topic sentence. Paragraphing, therefore, divides your essay up into convenient units that your reader will be able to understand without losing interest.

> Cardamon is a strong-smelling spice used extensively in oriental cooking. Native to India and southeastern Asia, the fruit is a small capsule containing eight to sixteen brown seeds. When roasted and crushed, these add an attractive flavour to curries. Indian and Malay curries make much use of the spice.

Note that all the sentences relate to the topic sentence: Cardamon is a strong-smelling spice used extensively in oriental cooking.

Now consider this student's paragraph:

> The concept of the head of state as a god-king flourished in the new kingdoms. It is said to have originated with the Devaraja cult, which in India took the form of worshipping the rulers while they lived and attributing some divine features to them. In Indonesia, the rulers took this a step further: they encouraged the belief that they were actually reincarnations of the gods Vishnu, Siva or Buddha and thus were to be given the respect and obedience due to them as gods.

Note that all the sentences in this paragraph are linked to the topic sentence containing the key idea 'the king as god'.

A common fault is to write what looks like a paragraph but is really only a jumble of unrelated ideas.

Study the following paragraph. Underline the sentence that does not belong; that does not relate to the idea or statement that the frog helps humans in many ways.

> The common frog aids humans in many ways. It controls insect pests in woods, farms and gardens. From the earliest times, the frog has been widely used as food. Many people dislike their looks and the feel of their skin. The frog is also widely used in scientific experiments.

The sentence that does not belong is, 'Many people . . . .'

Paragraphing

Now study this paragraph:

> One of the most important aspects of the new kingdoms was the concept of the head of state as a god-king. The Hinduized states of Indonesia relied very heavily on taxes derived from maritime trade. Many of these states did not last long but succumbed to more powerful rivals. Factional rivalries among the nobility also weakened the states.

Underline the topic sentence. Do all the sentences relate to the topic sentence?
This paragraph is about:

- the head of state as a god-king?
- state economics?
- the weaknesses of many states?

You are not sure, because **this is not a paragraph**, merely a collection of unrelated sentences. It happens to look like a paragraph. It's punctuated like a paragraph. But it's not a unit — it's a mess. The topic sentence mentions the concept of the god-king, but the other sentences deal with entirely different issues.

Consider this paragraph, taken from a third-year history essay:

> The Mappilia muslims live in the narrow belt along the southwest coast of India, with the population concentrated in the State of Kerala. Relatively isolated, they developed a unique Mappila language and culture. As stated previously, the Mappilas had a history of rebellions and outbreaks of violence as far back as the eighteenth century. The principal causes seem to stem from agrarian suffering, poverty and resentment towards the British, all inflamed by religious fanaticism.

- Is it a good paragraph?
- What is the paragraph about? Underline the topic sentence.
- Do all the sentences relate to the topic sentence?

Stop! Don't read any further just yet. Consider these two questions again.

67

You Can Write

Now read on:

A poor paragraph. There are two very different topics: the nature of the Mappila Muslims, and the Mappila muslim rebellions.

This type of poor paragraphing is a major weakness in student writing. It is usually caused by inadequate or poor planning.

Planning in the early stages will help prevent you writing non-paragraphs.

Length of paragraphs

Because of poor planning, some students write paragraphs that are either too long or too short. A very rough guide is that essay paragraphs should be about 100–200 words long, containing about four to seven sentences. Paragraphs longer or shorter than this may well be effective. However, very long paragraphs will cause your reader to lose concentration and obscure your meaning, while very short paragraphs will irritate.

Single- or two-sentence paragraphs should only be used to create a special (usually dramatic) effect.

Single-sentence paragraphs are used in other kinds of writing, such as newspaper reports, when the author wishes to convey information in as vivid a fashion as possible. While this is a very successful technique for newspaper writing, the same technique in the longer essay will unsettle the reader.

Imagine a long essay paragraphed like this:

> One of the most important aspects of the new kingdoms was the concept of the head of state as a god-king.
> This is said to have originated from the Devaraja cult, which in India took the form of worshipping the rulers while they lived and attributing some divine features to them.
> In Indonesia the rulers took this a step further.
> They encouraged the belief that they were actually reincarnations of the gods Vishnu, Siva or Buddha and thus

were to be given the respect and obedience due to them as gods.

By the end of the essay you would be thoroughly confused and fed-up. Short paragraphs are effective in newspapers, which are divided into narrow columns. In essays, however, they create a choppy, irritating effect. On the other hand, monstrously long paragraphs will send your reader to sleep. A reader's ability to comprehend the material rapidly falls off in a very long paragraph. Pick out a very long paragraph in one of your references and note how your concentration tends to fade after about fifteen lines. The same will happen when someone reads *your* long paragraphs.

Each paragraph should relate to the central idea or theme of the essay.

If your paragraph does not seem to fit in, you may have to throw it away. Don't forget, however, that background information may be necessary; just don't let it dominate the essay.

Each paragraph should be linked to the one before and the one after.

Since the function of paragraphing is to assist the reader, you should try to make your essay flow. Your reader should have the feeling that each paragraph serves a function and that it develops from the previous paragraph and leads into the next. This flow occurs naturally in a well-organised essay. When you have had practice in essay writing, you will make most of the links without thinking.

Check on paragraph flow at the revision stage. You will probably have to do some reorganisation: you may need to omit a paragraph, consolidate two smaller paragraphs into one, or add a further explanatory paragraph.

How to link paragraphs

1 *Proper planning*

The links will often result quite naturally from your organisation.

You Can Write

2 *Repetition*

One device you may use occasionally to link paragraphs is repetition. Repeat a word or phrase from the last sentence of the paragraph in the first sentence in the new paragraph, as in these examples:

> ... the members of the new Whitlam Government at the end of 1972.
> That government initiated the process ... .

(from a magazine)

> ... seventy per cent of scheduled tribe families have been alienated from their land by way of mortgage.
> But avaricious moneylenders cannot be held responsible for all instances of land alienation.

(from a second-year student)

> ... importance attached to the god-king certainly originated with the emergence of so-called Hinduized kingdoms.
> The term 'Hinduized' is commonly used ... .

(from a first-year student)

3 *Use signpost words*

Signpost words are used to link sentences.
For example:

> As workers, Australians have many fine traits. They are generally easy to get on with, and seldom temperamental. *In addition*, they are direct and straightforward. *Nevertheless*, they have some failings. They do not, *for example*, work as hard as people from many other countries.

Signpost words are also useful for linking paragraphs.
Common signpost words:

> admittedly, consequently, furthermore, however, in addition, in fact, moreover, nevertheless, of course, on the other hand, therefore, thus.

In the following, underline the signpost words that link the sentences and paragraphs. What do they tell the reader?

Paragraphing

> Cancer terrifies most people. A wild form of growth that destroys life if unchecked, it was known and feared in ancient Egypt, Greece and India. Today, as then, it strikes individuals of all ages and all socioeconomic groups. The alleged high mortality rate of cancer victims has induced in many people an obsessive dread.
> In addition, some forms of treatment are seen as almost worse than the cancer itself. Radical surgery sometimes disfigures. Radiation therapy can destroy healthy as well as diseased tissue. Chemotherapy — treatment with drugs — can have appalling side-effects. Moreover, none of these treatments guarantees a permanent cure.
> On the other hand, many cancers can be successfully treated. Almost 92 per cent of patients survive longer than five years after being treated for skin cancer. Even more deadly forms of cancer can be cured if treated early enough. Surgical cure rates for breast cancer range between 47 and 82 per cent, depending on the extent of the cancer at the time of surgery.
> By altering his or her eating habits and cutting out smoking, an individual can lessen the chances of getting cancer. Cancer no longer deserves the terrible reputation as an untreatable killer.

The signpost 'In addition . . .' tells the reader that you are continuing with the same argument: the reasons why people fear cancer. The signpost 'On the other hand . . .' tells the reader that you are about to provide a more positive view: developments in cancer cure and prevention.

You should not overuse signposts, but they can be very useful, particularly when you are going to consider an entirely new point or an alternative viewpoint and want to signal to the reader that a change in course is coming.

4 Headings

As a general rule, avoid headings in short, formal, undergraduate academic essays; they are best kept for long essays (over 3000 words) and for reports. In a short essay, they irritate the reader, although lecturers sometimes encourage their use to help inexperienced writers organise

71

their material. If you find it helpful to use them in your first draft, do so, but cut them out when you revise.

I repeat: if you **plan** your essay, most of the paragraph links will be made quite naturally. One paragraph will lead on to the next. You will only need consciously to use repetition or signpost words when you are working on the final draft(s).

6 Developing your Argument

In many essays, you will be asked to develop an argument. The aim of argument is to win people over to your view by appealing to their reason. Sound argument is based on fact, not opinion. The following will help you develop your ability to argue logically and clearly. Practice in writing essays will sharpen your skills still further, especially if you take careful note of your lecturers' comments, suggestions and criticisms. You won't improve very much if you simply glance at the grade the lecturers award and ignore their comments on your essays.

1 Provide evidence and examples

In order to convince your reader that your argument is sound, you will need to provide evidence and examples; assertion — a statement made without evidence — is never enough. Whether you are analysing a play, or discussing the merits of a theory of psychology, or explaining why a particular event in history occurred, you will need to provide **evidence**. For most essays, you must find your evidences in **sources** (such as books, journals, newspapers) other than your textbooks. As well as demonstrating by referencing (see next chapter) that you have read the sources, you must also give **examples** to support your argument. If, for example, you are arguing that the Australian Senate has blocked Labor Party legislation more consistently than that of non-Labor governments, then you should provide **evidence** by using **examples**. Stating that somebody else says this is so is not really enough.

One of the most frequent criticisms of students' essays is their lack of supporting **evidence**. You need sound,

You Can Write

detailed evidence to support or refute a point of view. You should distinguish between your opinion (what you believe to be true) and what you can prove. Lecturers get tired of writing: 'Give an example,' 'Discuss further,' 'What evidence do you have for this statement?'.
So, as well as referencing fully and correctly, you must also give examples.
Consider this sentence:

> Since 1945, the Australian Senate has prevented the Labor Party from governing effectively by persistently failing to pass important legislation.

As it stands, this is merely an **assertion**: you believe it to be true, but you provide no evidence.

Assertions (statement made without supporting evidence) **are very weak. They do not convince.**

Now let's strengthen your argument:

> Since 1945, the Australian Senate has prevented the Labor Party from governing effectively by persistently failing to pass important legislation (see Brown: 1975: 28; Smith 1982: 34–36).

This is better! Now the eminent scholars Brown and Smith, who have spent all their lives studying Australian politics, support you. You've got a much stronger case. But it's still weak. What if the reader says that Brown and Smith are biased or are fools? You can strengthen your argument still further. *Like this*:

> Since 1945, the Australian Senate has prevented the Labor Party from governing effectively by persistently blocking important legislation (see Brown 1975: 28; Smith 1982: 34–36). For instance, in 1974 the Senate blocked eighty pieces of important legislation (Smith 1982: 33). McGuire's (1981: 42) analysis of Senate voting between 1950 and 1980 shows that the Senate blocked 850 Labor bills but only five of the non-Labor party bills.

Now your argument is much stronger. You've given some

facts. You've provided some evidence. You've used examples. You've used a range of sources. **Provide examples, referenced if possible, to support your statements.** Statistics, in particular, can be effectively used to support your argument.

2 Define important terms fully

A further major weakness in many student arguments is the failure to define important terms or to define them adequately. Words have different meanings for different people and different disciplines. For example, if you are discussing the Australian feminist movement's influence on Australian politics, you must, at some stage (preferably early in the essay) define what you mean by the Australian feminist movement: a group of professional women? any group of women concerned with women's interests? women who belong to specific women's organisations? and so on. If you don't clearly define your key terms, then how can you argue? You might, for example, state that the feminist movement has consistently supported the Labor Party. If you have not defined the movement, your reader might ask: 'What about the various women's groups associated with the non-Labor parties?'. You are immediately on the defensive. You may have excluded these groups in your own mind, but without clear definitions your argument can easily be challenged.

Some terms, of course, are very difficult to define, especially in the Social Sciences. For example, the question, 'What is class?', is the subject of many books and of violent debate among academics. The best thing you can do with a difficult term is to find out how your lecturer defines it or, failing that, to go to your text book or a specialised dictionary or encyclopedia.

You only need to define the **key terms**, particularly those that appear in the essay question and are crucial to your argument. You would not be able to write anything at all if you had to define everything. Just be careful that you are as clear as possible when using the major **key terms**.

You Can Write

3 Avoid sweeping generalisations

'All', and words like it, should be used very carefully, if at all. Things are seldom 'all', 'every' or 'always'.

>All Russians are communists.
>Every human society is based on exploitation.
>All Asians are hard working.
>All politicians are greedy.
>It is a well-known fact that people are always looking for change.
>All union bosses are power-hungry.
>Everyone knows that students are irresponsible.

You leave yourself wide open to criticism when you use 'all' or its equivalents, such as 'every' and 'always' (or even when you only imply them).

4 Consider both sides of the argument

You cannot simply ignore important arguments or evidence that challenges your argument. Raise them before your reader does, preferably early in the essay, and refute them as best as you can. This is where wide reading and thinking about what you have read are important. You may be able to find enough evidence to dismiss or perhaps to weaken the other argument or evidence. You may even wish to concede a point so long as it doesn't destroy your argument.

5 Be critical of your references

Students straight from school find it hard to criticise their sources or their lecturers. The school-learning process has often conditioned them to repeat uncritically what their teacher or textbook says. Moreover, some academics inhibit students from challenging them or their particular views of the world.

Of course, developing and sharpening your critical ability takes time. You need to have some background knowledge before you can start challenging the authorities in the field.

For a start, you can simply accept that:

Developing your Argument

- Your lecturers and the authors you read are subject to the same human failings as anybody else.
- Ideas change, and old theories are discarded.
- New evidence emerges that refutes earlier arguments.

Try to be aware of various viewpoints and biases, including your own. If you know, for example, that your lecturer is a member of the local branch of the Liberal or Labor Party, then you should keep this in mind when he or she talks about Australian politics. Ask yourself whether the lecturer backs up statements and assertions. He or she may be completely even-handed and fair but, on the other hand, may not be. Do not accept every statement uncritically; use your own judgement and analytical skills in the classroom as elsewhere.

Before reading a book in detail, find out as much as you can about the book's author. The preface or dust-jacket will often give you useful information. The more eminent scholars will appear in biographical encyclopedias — ask a reference librarian for help. An extremely good way of learning to be critical is to read the book reviews. (See chapter 10.) These will alert you to the sorts of debate in which academics engage — and also show you that even so-called experts can often be very stupid and petty. After all, they're only human!

6 Check your assumptions

An assumption is something that you take for granted. Sometimes assumptions are stated; more often they are hidden.

Some of the sorts of assumptions that people hold:

- To analyse literature is to kill it.
- Progress is good.
- The newest is best.
- If it is printed in a book it must be true.
- Societies function for the good of the majority.
- Only the fittest survive.
- Most politicians are dedicated, hard-working servants of the people.

- Shakespeare is beyond criticism.

Hidden assumptions can prevent us from seeing alternative viewpoints or from developing a more sophisticated argument.
For example:
> What are the duties and responsibilities of members of parliament?

If you accept the assumption 'that politicians pass legislation to help govern the country', you would answer this question by detailing the party system, the sorts of legislation passed, and so on.

If you reject this assumption and hold that 'the Cabinet members make all the important decisions', you would allot a much more limited role to the ordinary members of parliament.

If you hold the assumption that powerful vested interests control society, then you would approach the question differently again, perhaps by being very critical of the value of parliament and, perhaps, parliamentarians.

Consider another example:
> A woman's place is in the home. Discuss.

If your assumption is 'that women should have the same opportunities as men', your argument would look at how certain institutions have prevented women from expanding their roles outside the home. If your assumption is 'that women are different from, or inferior to, men' (which, of course, you might hold quite unconsciously), then you would attempt to define the differences, stress the importance of their role as mothers and wives, refer to other societies, and so on.

7 *Develop your skills to reason clearly and logically*

Throughout your tertiary studies, you will be developing skills in reasoning clearly and logically. One skill you will need is to pick out fallacies (errors or weaknesses) in

Developing your Argument

argument. The following are the more common fallacies that you will meet.

A The 'either-or' fallacy

This states that things are either black or white. (In fact, they may well be grey.)

> If you do not support the Russians over the Olympic boycott, then you must support the American stance.

B The red herring

In fox hunting, a strong-smelling red herring is dragged across the fox's trail to confuse the hounds. In argument, the **red herring** occurs when you bring in an irrelevant side-issue.

> Why should we try to persuade people to stop smoking? After all, alcohol causes even worse medical and social problems. (The argument is about banning cigarettes; the alcohol problem is a **red herring**.)

C Personal abuse

This fallacy consists of attacking the person's character, not his position or argument.

> The Minister for Health is hopeless at his job. Have you seen him? He is very fat, drinks heavily and smokes 100 cigarettes a day.
> (He could still be a very efficient minister.)

D The bandwagon fallacy

This fallacy consists of stating that an argument must be valid because most people support it.

> Most Australians favour a reduction in income tax. Reducing income tax, therefore, must be good for the majority of Australians.
> (It may be, but just because most people think that it will doesn't prove anything.)

E Begging the question

You assume in your statement that what you are arguing

has already been proved.

> This essential legislation must be implemented. (You haven't proved it is essential.)

F Confusing cause and effect

You assume that because one event followed another, the one caused the other.

> Many Australian states abolished the death penalty. Since then, crimes of violence have increased dramatically. Abolishing the death penalty has, therefore, caused an increase in the crime rate.
> (There may be other more important factors.)

G Sweeping generalisation

This fallacy misuses statistics. It makes a broad generalisation on the basis of an unrepresentative or too small sample.

> This make of car is no good. I've had a great deal of trouble with it. Nobody I know likes it. Even the mechanic at the local garage thinks it's a lemon.

Which fallacies do the following illustrate?

1 The union case is immoral. Unions today are far too greedy. When I was young, I worked 48 hours a week for very low wages.
2 In a recent poll, most people favoured a reduction in migration to Australia. This proves that migration is bad for Australia.
3 Over the past few years, more marriages have ended in divorce. Recent figures show that juvenile crime has increased dramatically. The breakdown of the institution of the family, therefore, has led to an increase in crime among young people.
4 The Democrats are sure to win the next election; all my friends are going to vote for the Democrat candidates.
5 What would a bigoted, racist, fascist mongrel like that know about land rights?

Developing your Argument

6 Why should men be given custody of children? Many of them have an alcohol problem and end up in jail.
7 The bible is divinely inspired; it says so in the third chapter of Timothy.
8 Either doctors must have complete freedom to set their own scale of fees or they will end up as public servants working for wages.

Answers:
1 Red herring. (What happened a long time ago is irrelevant.)
2 Bandwagon fallacy. (Because some people want a reduction in migration, that does not prove migration is bad for the country.)
3 Confusing cause and effect. (There may be no relationship between the two social changes.)
4 Sweeping generalisation. (The sample is too small.)
5 Personal abuse. (Attacking the man, not the argument.)
6 Red herring. (The alcohol problem has nothing to do with the question of custody.)
7 Begging the question. (You can't *prove* that the bible is divinely inspired because the bible says it is.)
8 Either-or fallacy. (There are other options.)

Develop your ability and confidence to query, to criticise and to construct your own logical arguments. After all, isn't that what education is all about?

7 Punctuating

Why punctuate?

Writing is different from speaking. When you speak, you quite unconsciously give your reader all sorts of clues as to what you mean: you raise or lower your voice; you pause; you use body language — you sit in a certain way, you wave your hands about, your facial expression changes. Writing is much more artificial. It is colder and more calculated. But that is one of its advantages. What may seem very reasonable and sensible when spoken may often be recognised as rubbish when written. The written word can be analysed much more easily than the spoken word. However, in order to write correctly and effectively, you need to learn certain techniques. One of the most important of these is the art of **punctuation**.

What is punctuation?

Punctuation is putting in the **stops** and **pauses** (commas, full stops, colons, semicolons, dashes and brackets) in your writing. You punctuate to help your reader understand. Leave out the punctuation and look what happens:

> Writing is different from speaking when you speak you quite unconsciously give your reader all sorts of clues as to what you mean you raise or lower your voice you pause you use body language you sit in a certain way you wave your hands about your facial expression changes writing is much more artificial it is colder and more calculated but that is one of its advantages what may seem very reasonable and sensible when spoken may often be recognised as rubbish when written the written word can be analysed much more easily than the

spoken word in order to write correctly and effectively you need to learn certain techniques one of the most important of these is the art of **punctuation**

Confusing?

To write well, you must learn to punctuate. Once you know how to punctuate, you will write more clearly, directly and confidently.

Let's clear up one misconception straightaway. Learning to punctuate is not about learning rules for their own sake; punctuation is about helping your reader understand you. Punctuation, therefore, is about **logic** and **reason** and about **consideration** for your reader. Once you understand the logic of punctuation, you will be able to punctuate much more confidently and precisely.

Before you can punctuate, you need to be able to do three things:

- **Recognise a *sentence*.**
- **Pick out the set (or sets) of *key words* (the most important words) within the sentence.**
- **Pick out the set (or sets) of supporting words within the sentence.**

You will also need to learn a few terms. You may have come across them before, but I'll assume that you haven't. These terms are not important by themselves, but you need to know them so that I can communicate with you. Take it easy. Work slowly, and build up your confidence.

You Can Write

A solid grounding in basic punctuation skills is essential if you want to write well.

Step one: recognise a sentence

- A sentence is the *basic unit* **of** writing.
- A sentence is *complete*.
- A sentence *makes sense*.
- Most sentences make a *statement*.

(A sentence may also ask a question or give a command, but we can ignore those for now.)
These are all sentences:

>The men killed their enemies.
>He went to Perth, but she stayed at work.
>Although he was ill, he ran the race.
>It was a hot day yesterday.
>Joan died.
>The microscope, introduced by van Leeuwenhoek, made possible the study of disease-causing organisms.

A sentence must contain at least one subject group and one verb group.

1 A subject group

A word or group of words that answers the question **who**? or **what**?

>John hit Bill.
>**Who?**
>Subject group — **John**
>The frightened dog bit the boy.
>**What?**
>Subject group — **The frightened dog**
>The man in the chair watched television.
>**Who?**
>Subject group — **The man in the chair**
>The wood was chopped by John.
>**What?**
>Subject group — **The wood**
>English sailors who were fond of the juice of lemons or limes did not succumb to scurvy.

Who?
Subject group — **English sailors who were fond of the juice of lemons or limes**

2 *A verb group*

A word or group of words that contains the **verb**, the word or group of words that tells you what is happening. A **verb** denotes action (ran) or state of being (the verb 'to be' and its parts, 'was', 'is', 'am', 'are', 'will be', etc.)

The plane crashed into the sea.
Verb group — **Crashed into the sea**
(Verb: **Crashed**)
Terry jumped over the fence.
Verb group — **Jumped over the fence**
(Verb: **Jumped**)
Ms Smith is the new president.
(Verb: **Is**)
Verb group — **Is the new president**

The parts of the verb 'to be' can also be combined with other verbs:

The flowers *will be sent* to her.
He *is going* to Perth.

A sentence may have more than one subject group and one verb group.

John went to Perth, but Pauline stayed at work.

Here we have one sentence containing what are, in effect, two sentences, joined by 'but'. Each could form a complete sentence on its own if you wished.
For example:

John went to Perth. Pauline stayed at work.

Another example:

The pressure increased, yet the boiler did not explode.

Again, you have two sentences joined together by 'yet' to form one sentence. You could make two complete sentences if you wished by putting a full stop after 'increased' and leaving out the 'yet'.

You Can Write

Now let's consolidate. Memorise the following:

A sentence must:

- **Make a complete (full) statement; make sense: be complete in itself.**
- **Contain at** *least* **one subject group and one verb group.**

You must be able to pick out a sentence before you can punctuate correctly.

Let's take a few examples:

> To the park.

This is obviously not a sentence.
It doesn't make sense by itself. It is incomplete.
It has no subject group.
It has no verb group.
It is only a **sentence fragment; an unfinished sentence**.
'He went to the park' is a sentence, but 'to the park' is only a fragment or part of the sentence.

> As he came in.

It contains a subject group (he).
It contains a verb group (came in).
But it is *not complete*. It is only part of something. It is a **sentence fragment**. It is not a sentence.
Something else needs to be added, e.g. 'As he came in, his son was leaving the house'.

> The house will be painted next week.

It contains a subject group (the house).
It contains a verb group (will be painted next week).
It makes a statement. It is complete.
It is a sentence.

> While the plane landed.

It contains a subject group (plane).
It contains a verb group (landed).
But it is not complete.
One feels that something else needs to be added before it is complete, e.g., 'While the plane landed, the custom officials

prepared to check the passengers' baggage'.
'While the plane landed' is, therefore, only a **sentence fragment**.

>The infection spread, so the patient died.

It makes sense.
It is complete.
It is a sentence.
You could, if you wished, break it into two sentences:
'The infection spread.' 'The patient died.'
You've got the choice.

>Not to mention reduction in exhaust pollutants.

It is not complete.
It has no subject group, so it is a **sentence fragment**.
We now know that:

A sentence must be complete and must contain at least one subject group and one verb group.

A sentence fragment is a word or groups of words that are only part of a sentence. They don't make a complete statement by themselves.

See if you can pick out the sentences from the sentence fragments. Be honest with yourself. Don't check the answer until you have finished. Remember the sentence must be complete. You shouldn't feel that you have to add something to finish it off.

1 The man lit a fire.
2 Although it was cold.
3 Although it was cold, he stripped off his clothes.
4 As the burglar ran around the corner.
5 The caste system is unique to India.
6 Reports that Marco Polo had arrived in India were not believed in Venice.
7 The blood level was determined by the technician.
8 If you are to be examined on the work of the previous year.
9 After the Japanese took up the serious study of the classics of Chinese philosophy.

You Can Write

10 The ease with which electrical energy can be changed into other forms of energy is one of the main reasons for its usefulness.

Answers:
1 Sentence complete.   2 Sentence fragment not complete. ('Although it was cold, I went for a jog.')   3 Sentence.   4 Sentence fragment. ('As the burglar ran around the corner, the police arrived from the other direction.')   5 Sentence. (Remember that 'is', 'was', 'am', 'are' are verbs.)   6 Sentence.   7 Sentence.   8 Sentence fragment.   9 Sentence fragment.   10 Sentence.

Sentences have nothing to do with length.

A sentence can be very short:

> John cried.
> (It is complete. It has a subject group and a verb group.)

By contrast, a sentence fragment can be very long:

> As he came out the door, his keys in his pocket and a surprised expression on his face, he saw standing near his car. (This is not complete. It's not finished. He saw? Put in 'a man' and it's a sentence.)

What seem like long sentences are often, in fact, only sentence fragments. This is another reason for not writing very long sentences.

Step two: pick out the set (or sets) of key words within the sentence

A set is simply a group of related things.

In every sentence you will find a **set** (group) or **sets** (groups) of words — the **key words** — which control or dominate the meaning of the sentence. (I use the term **key words**. In other books you will find different terms for the same set of words. What you call them is not important. You only need to recognise them.)

Each set of **key words** must contain a subject group and a verb group.

The **key words** may by themselves form a complete sentence:

> Tom hit the big boy.

Punctuating

The **key words** may be a part — the most important part — of a sentence:

> Although he was small, <u>Tom lifted the heavy weight</u>.
> If it is fine, <u>he will go to Perth</u>.
> <u>The rocket reached the moon</u>, in spite of a faulty computer.

There may be more than one set of **key words** in a sentence:

> <u>Tom hit Bill</u>, but <u>he was not punished</u>.
> (This, of course, could be written as two sentences: '<u>Tom hit Bill</u>.' '<u>He was not punished</u>.')

You can have any combination of the above:

> Although he was small, <u>Tom hit Bill</u>, but <u>he was soon knocked flat on his back</u>.

Identifying the key words is the secret to punctuation.

Once you can pick out the set or sets of **key words** in a sentence, you will be able to punctuate confidently.
*Underline the set or sets of **key words** in the following*:

1 Spinning out of control, the car hit the pedestrian.
2 The car hit the pedestrian, but the driver was not arrested by the police.
3 Because my brother is a panel-beater, we decided to buy the car.
4 You should be pleased with the team, for it has won three games.
5 Mary and Sue went to the beach; Sharon stayed at home.
6 Although he was ill, he went to work.
7 The death rate for pneumonia has been reduced considerably by the use of sulfa drugs.
8 However, as Albert Einstein has shown, the mass of a body does not actually remain constant.

Answers:
1 Spinning out of control, <u>the car hit the pedestrian</u>.
2 <u>The car hit the pedestrian</u>, but <u>the driver was not arrested by the police</u>. (Two sets of key words.)
3 Because my brother is a panel-beater, <u>we decided to buy the car</u>.
4 <u>You should be pleased with the team</u>, for <u>it has won three games</u>. (Two sets of key words.)

89

You Can Write

5 Mary and Sue went to the beach; Sharon stayed at home. (Two sets of key words.)
6 Although he was ill, he went to work.
7 The death rate for pneumonia has been reduced considerably by the use of sulfa drugs.
8 However, as Albert Einstein has shown, the mass of a body does not actually remain constant.

(Look at the punctuation above. Can you see a pattern emerging? You will find it useful to go through sentences picking out the **key words** either by yourself or in a group.)
You now should be able to:

- **recognise a sentence**
- **recognise the set (or sets) of key words within the sentence.**

Step three: pick out the supporting word (or set of supporting words) that assist the key words in the sentence

These provide additional information within the sentence but are totally dependent upon the **key words**.
 They can be omitted and the sentence will still have the same basic meaning.
For example:

    Although I was ill, I came to work.

Key words: I came to work.
Supporting words: Although I was ill.

    In spite of the danger, the woman rescued her family.

Key words: The woman rescued her family.
Supporting words: In spite of the danger.

    The boy ran the full marathon distance, although he was tired.

Key words: The boy ran the full marathon distance.
Supporting words: Although he was tired.

    As Albert Einstein has shown, the mass of a body does not actually remain constant.

Key words: The mass of a body does not actually remain constant.

Punctuating

Supporting words: As Albert Einstein has shown.
Some supporting words act as **signposts**. They help show the connection between one sentence and another. They help the reader by telling him or her which way the argument or discussion is going ('however'; 'therefore'; 'on the other hand'; 'for this reason'; 'finally'; 'of course'; 'indeed', etc.). They also can let the reader know that you are continuing along the same road ('similarly', 'therefore', 'consequently', 'likewise') or that you are changing course ('on the other hand, 'however').

<u>However</u>, I agree with your decision.
The boy, <u>however</u>, was late.
<u>Indeed</u>, you are already too late.
The ship, <u>in fact</u>, was sunk last week.
<u>Consequently</u>, we can see how important sociology is for understanding human society.
<u>On the other hand</u>, management theory now argues that the human factor is important.

Underline the supporting word or set of supporting words in the following:

1 Although I was late, the lecturer welcomed me.
2 We went immediately to the police station.
3 Of course, we went immediately to the police station.
4 Four or five readings and recitations are usually required.
5 In my experience, four or five readings and recitations are usually required.
6 The first revision, then, should take place as soon as possible after the original learning.
7 As you know, I sold my business last year after I had two coronaries.
8 You must, however, keep your work up-to-date.
9 Secondly, he was far too occupied with the serious task of consolidating his authority in Arabia.
10 The ship, although it was sinking, was not abandoned by the crew.
 (Again, look at the punctuation. Can you pick out a pattern?)

You Can Write

Answers:
1 <u>Although I was late</u>   2 (None)   3 <u>Of course</u>   4 (None)   5 <u>In my experience</u>   6 <u>then</u>   7 <u>As you know</u>   8 <u>however</u>   9 <u>Secondly</u>   10 <u>although it was sinking</u>

Now that you can:

- **recognise a sentence**
- **recognise the key words within the sentence**
- **recognise the supporting word or set of supporting words within the sentence**

you have the basis for punctuating confidently.

You need to know three punctuation rules:

Punctuation rule one: do not use punctuation to break up the key words. Keep them together as a unit

Why?

The **key words** contain the essential meaning. The reader should be able to pick them out quickly.

You use punctuation to let your reader know which the key words are. In other words, you use punctuation to show your reader the **key words**.

> The elements combined in the tube.
> (Correct punctuation. The key words are kept together.)

These would be wrong:

> The elements, combined in the tube.
> The elements combined. In the tube.
> The; elements combined in the tube.

In each case you have broken up the **key words** for no reason. **Don't do this.** You will confuse the reader if you do. The reader (either consciously or unconsciously) is looking for the **key words**. Remember that they contain the most important information. Use punctuation to help him or her find them quickly.

Sometimes you will want to insert a supporting word or set of supporting words within your **key words**. This is quite

Punctuating

acceptable. Punctuate (using commas) to help the reader separate or distinguish the set of **key words** from the set of **supporting words**.

> Tom ran to Perth.
> Tom, although he was ill, ran to Perth.
> Tom, therefore, ran to Perth.
> The experiment, in fact, was a failure.

If you think about it, this is really not an exception at all to the rule that you must not break up **key words**. The punctuation (the pair of commas) tells the reader that what is between the commas does not belong to the key words.

The *only* time that you punctuate within the key words is when you use commas in a list of things.

> He was a tall, happy person.
> We bought timber, tools, nails and paint.
> He saw the long, sleek, grey ship.

State whether these are correctly punctuated, and underline the key words:

1 The man dropped his hat.
2 Shipments, are to be made on Saturday.
3 Shipments, however are to be made on Saturday.
4 These models, for example, were sold very early.
5 We bought fruit, vegetables and meat.
6 I maintain that, objectivity, in science, is a myth.
7 I maintain, moreover, that objectivity in science is a myth.
8 We increased prices, therefore, to cover the cost.
9 For this reason, gases do not have any specific volume.
10 The human heart, contrary to popular belief, is not on the left side of the chest.

Answers:
 1 Correct. The man dropped his hat.
 2 Incorrect. Shipments are to be made on Saturday.
 3 Incorrect. 'However' is not part of the set of **key words**. You must use a **pair** of commas to mark it off. Shipments, however, are to be made on Saturday.
 4 Correct. These models, for example, were sold very early.

93

You Can Write

5 Correct. No need for a comma after vegetables. <u>We bought fruit, vegetables and meat.</u> A list.
6 Incorrect. 'in science' is part of the set of **key words**.
 I maintain that objectivity in science is a myth.
7 Correct. 'Moreover' is not part of the set of **key words**. <u>I maintain, moreover, that objectivity in science is a myth.</u>
8 Correct. <u>We increased prices</u>, therefore, <u>to cover the cost.</u>
9 Correct. <u>For this reason,</u> <u>gases do not have any specific volume.</u>
10 Correct. <u>The human heart</u>, contrary to popular belief, <u>is not on the left side of the chest.</u>

Write Punctuation Rule One here. Then, check your answer.

....
....
....

Punctuation rule two: keep the sets (groups) of key words apart from each other by punctuation

Choose the appropriate one of these:

- **a full stop**
- **a semicolon**
- **a colon**
- **a dash**
- **a comma** *plus* **a joining word ('for', 'and', 'nor', 'but', 'or', 'yet', 'so').**

For example:

<u>The tall man ran out of the door;</u> <u>the small lady entered through the window.</u>
<u>The tall man ran out the door</u>, but <u>he missed the bus.</u>
<u>The tall man ran out the door.</u> <u>He missed the bus.</u>

The comma by itself is the only form of punctuation that is too weak to keep the key words apart.

This is incorrect punctuation:

<u>The tall man ran out the door,</u> <u>the small lady met him outside.</u>

Using a comma *by itself* to keep **key words** apart is an error known as the **comma splice**. The comma is used specifically to separate the supporting words from the **key words** in a sentence.

> Although he was late, he managed to pass the exam.

We need a stronger form of punctuation clearly to separate the **key words**. Remember that the reader must be able to pick out the **key words** quickly. We have a number of options to keep the **key words** apart.
If we want to make two separate sentences, we use a **full stop**.

> Susan went to class. Tom stayed in bed.

If we want to join two sentences, we have a number of options.

> Susan went to class, but Tom stayed in bed. (a comma *plus* a **joining word**, 'but')
> Susan went to class; Tom stayed in bed.

(We shall see in the next chapter how to use the different forms of punctuation.)
This is incorrect:

> Susan went to class, Tom stayed in bed.

This error is an example of the ....
An error very similar to the **comma splice** is where you don't punctuate at all between **key words**.

> Tom went to class he forgot his paper.

This error is called the **run-on sentence** because one sentence runs into the next.

Remember you must keep the key words apart from each other by a pause stronger than a comma.

Mark these correct or incorrect. If the latter, name the error. (If you are not sure, underline the **key words**.)

1 Gandhi was India's greatest leader. He died just after India became independent.

You Can Write

2 Sociology is an important subject many students do not take it.
3 Sociology is an important subject, but many students do not take it.
4 Some students find sociology difficult, they find that the subject is too abstract.
5 Some students find physics difficult. They find the basic concepts difficult to grasp.
6 Genghis Khan was a ruthless leader, his followers loved him.
7 The German invasion of Russia was a grave error. Hitler did not agree with this opinion.
8 History tells us about past events it helps us understand our own society.
9 Correct punctuation can easily be learnt, many students never bother to learn the art.
10 Semai women own the fields. Semai men are the leaders of the community.

Answers:
1 Correct. 2 Incorrect—run-on sentence. Note: **key words**. 'Sociology is an important subject. Many students do not take it. 3 Correct. Comma plus joining word. 4 Incorrect. Comma splice. 5 Correct. 6 Incorrect. Comma splice. 7 Correct. 8 Incorrect. Run-on sentence. 9 Incorrect. Comma splice. 10 Correct.

Write Punctuation Rule Two here. Then check your answer.

....

....

....

Punctuation rule three: be ready to use the comma (or brackets, dashes) to separate the set of key words from the supporting word or set of supporting words

    Although I was ill, I ran in the fun run.
    Hindu fanatics assassinated Gandhi, despite his being a devout Hindu.
    The man, although he was old, fought off his attackers.

Punctuating

> Therefore, he ran away.
> Sociology, therefore, is a most important subject.

You will notice that I am not as definite about this rule. **Punctuation is not about applying a set of rigid rules.** In some instances, there is no argument. For example, the comma splice *is* wrong. However, in many instances, especially where the comma is involved, you have the choice as to whether you punctuate or not. The secret of punctuation lies in you — the writer — fully understanding the basic principles.

Few people use commas either correctly or confidently. You will also find that writers nowadays use fewer commas than did writers in the past. ('Sociology therefore is a most difficult subject.' Many teachers would now argue that the commas around 'therefore' are not essential. But no one would argue that you can use only one comma in that sentence: it's a pair or nothing.) Most people know a few rules and can usually guess where to put in the commas, but that's not good enough if you want to write precise, clear English.

If you want to punctuate well:

- **You should be able to use the comma if *you* decide to do so. The comma can be a most useful weapon in your writing armoury.**
- **You must use the comma if leaving it out might confuse your reader.**

For example:

> When they married women relinquished all property to their husbands.

Insert a comma after 'married' and note how the uncertainty is immediately cleared up.

As a rough guide:

- **Use a comma if it is essential to clarify your meaning.**
- **Generally use the comma if the supporting word or set of words comes first in the sentence.** If you don't, the reader may not be sure where the supporting words end and the **key words** begin.

97

Despite his illness, he went to work.
On the other hand, he is a pleasant person.

- **Use the commas (you'll need a pair) if the supporting word or words fall inside the key words.**

  The ship, which had just emerged from the fog, fired upon the lifeboat.

- **Instead of commas you may wish to use a pair of brackets** if the set of supporting words is only of **slight** importance or could distract the reader.

  Mahatma Gandhi (the Father of Indian Independence) was, ironically, assassinated by Hindu fanatics.

  or

- **A pair of dashes** if you want to **emphasise** the set of supporting words.

  The battlefield — a scene of great carnage — was located close to Delhi.

Brackets and dashes are used far less often than commas. Make sure that you always use a matched pair — two commas, or two brackets, or two dashes. Don't mix them.

- **You can usually omit the comma if the set of supporting words comes last.**

There is much less chance of confusing your reader if the set of key words comes before the set of supporting words. However, you may sometimes wish to use the comma. Generally, you will use a comma if you wish to emphasise the set of supporting words that otherwise would melt into the control unit. (Now we're starting to make subtle use of punctuation.)

I ran a hard race in spite of my leg injury.
(This is quite correct. You're making a simple statement.)
I ran a hard race, in spite of my leg injury.
(This, again, is quite correct. You're drawing your reader's attention to your leg injury. In effect, you're asking for sympathy or praise.)

Punctuating

I ran a hard race — in spite of my leg injury.
(This is also correct, but now you're boasting. The dash highlights your achievement in racing hard with a leg injury. Don't use the dash very often, as it is too strong for normal writing. Overusing it will irritate the reader and weaken its effect.)

The comma is delicate. Most inexperienced writers either ignore it, worry about it, or use it indiscriminately. Yet, with practice, you can use it to strengthen your writing.

Summary: punctuation using commas
- **Always use a comma if it is essential to avoid confusion.**
- **Usually use a comma if the supporting word or set of supporting words comes first.**
- **Usually use a comma (you may occasionally wish to use brackets or dashes instead) if the supporting word or words fall within the key words.**
- **You may wish to use a comma if the supporting word or words come last, especially if you wish to emphasise them.**

Punctuate the following. Also, underline the key words.
Remember when using commas, you have much more choice. Consider the various options.

1 Although Hitler was insane he managed to dominate German politics.
2 Hitler although he was insane made some very wise decisions.
3 Hitler was a brilliant public speaker despite his high-pitched voice.
4 I ran in the race although I was ill.
   (Punctuate to show you are feeling very pleased with yourself.)
5 Consequently I expect you to complete the assignment although you have argued that you should not have to do so.
6 These models for example are defective.
7 His hopes dashed the man wept.
8 The burglar a great brute of a fellow charged out of the shop.
(Emphasise his huge size.)

99

You Can Write

9 I knew that I would be promoted despite my boss's disapproval.
(Punctuate to emphasise your victory.)
10 The new lecturer a good friend of mine strode into the room.
11 His boat however was damaged beyond repair.
12 If the object is moving faster shutter speeds are needed.

Some possibilities:
1 Although Hitler was insane, <u>he managed to dominate German politics</u>.
2 <u>Hitler</u>, although he was insane, <u>made some very wise decisions</u>.
or
<u>Hitler</u> — although he was insane — <u>made some very wise decisions</u>.
(You are emphasising his insanity.)
or
Hitler (although he was insane) <u>made some very wise decisions</u>.
(You are underplaying his insanity.)
3 <u>Hitler was a brilliant public speaker</u> despite his high-pitched voice.
(Correct. A comma is not essential if the support unit comes last, but you've got the option.)
or
<u>Hitler was a brilliant public speaker</u>, despite his high-pitched voice.
(Also correct. You tend to emphasise his high-pitched voice.)
or
<u>Hitler was a brilliant public speaker</u> — despite his high-pitched voice.
(Again correct. Now you are pointing out his high-pitched voice.)
4 <u>I ran in the race</u> — although I was ill. (comma after 'race' if you wish)
5 Consequently, <u>I expect you to complete the assignment</u>, although you have argued that you should not have to do so.
(or no comma after 'consequently' and 'assignment')
6 <u>These models</u>, for example, <u>are defective</u>.
7 His hopes dashed, <u>the man wept</u>.
(Without the comma, it reads initially as if the hopes dashed the man.)
8 <u>The burglar</u> — a great brute of a fellow — <u>charged out of the shop</u>.
(I'd use the dashes, although commas or brackets could be correct.)
9 <u>I knew that I would be promoted</u> — despite my boss's disapproval.
(Comma or no punctuation would change the emphasis.)
10 <u>The new lecturer</u> (a good friend of mine) <u>strode into the room</u>.
(You could use commas, but I prefer the brackets in this example.)
11 <u>His boat</u>, however, <u>was damaged beyond repair</u>.
12 If the object is moving, <u>faster shutter speeds are needed</u>.

You can see, therefore, that sometimes a set of supporting words will add additional information. The punctuation shows you which are the key words.

Punctuating

Examine the following carefully. Note the **key words** and punctuation.

The Prime Minister of Australia, Mr Hawke, held a press conference yesterday.
Louis Pasteur, a French scientist, gave his name to the process known as pasteurisation.
Mr Begin, apparently in good health, appeared in public for the first time in three months.
As with so many of the world's art treasures, the book was given up for lost.
The ushers had some trouble showing concertgoers to their seats, a problem that was little helped by several late arrivals.
The thymus gland, located at the base of the windpipe, seems to control growth during adolescence.
Located at the base of the windpipe, the thymus gland seems to control growth.
As a result of investigations begun by Amadeo Avogrado, it was discovered that a mole of any substance has the same number of molecules as a mole of any other substance.

Sometimes a set of supporting words attaches a condition to the key words.

If you do not come, I shall go on my own.
Unless I hear from you soon, I shall not mark your essay.
If there are more positive than negative charges, the body is positive.
If the condition of the Australian Aboriginals is to improve, the Australian Government will have to introduce new legislation.

If the logic of this escapes you, just remember to punctuate supporting units starting with 'if' or 'unless', especially if they start the sentence.

Warning about using commas with 'who'

You use commas to help your reader. **Misusing them and thereby confusing the reader is worse than not using them at all.** Don't just stick them in to make your writing look better. Use them quite deliberately. Don't overuse them.

101

You Can Write

You have learnt that a pair of commas separate the **key words** from the supporting word or set of supporting words. The commas tell the reader that the sentence will not substantially change in meaning if the words between the commas are left out. Look at the following example:

> John, who has just completed his master's degree, is off to America soon.

If the major point you are making is that your friend John is going to America, this punctuation is quite correct.

You mention that he has completed his degree, but the information is not vital. Leaving out 'who has just completed his master's degree' will not really change anything.

(Note: It is essential that you include **both** commas. The following would thoroughly confuse the reader: 'John who had just completed his master's degree, is off to America soon'.)

On the other hand, consider this sentence:

> Irishmen, who have criminal records, should not be allowed to migrate to Australia.

If you use the commas, you are saying that 'who have criminal records' can be omitted and the same meaning remains. So you are saying, 'Irishmen should not be allowed to migrate to Australia', when you really (I hope) only wanted to keep out those with criminal records. You've broken Punctuation Rule One: Never use punctuation to break up **key words**.

The **key words** are:

> <u>Irishmen who have criminal records should not be allowed to migrate to Australia.</u>

The subject of this sentence is: 'Irishmen who have criminal records'.

If you wish to say that 'boys who talk too much get on your nerves', don't punctuate like this:

> Boys, who never stop talking, get on my nerves.

Punctuating

The commas mean that the reader can leave out the 'who never stop talking'. Now you've become sexist: you have slandered all boys. 'Who never stop talking' in this instance belongs to the **key words**, and cannot be left out. The subject of the sentence is: 'Boys who never stop talking'. So:

Do not use commas if the words within the commas are essential for the meaning, that is if the meaning would change substantially if the words enclosed by the commas were left out.

Write Punctuation Rule Three here. Then, check your answer.

....

....

....

Fill in the blanks:

1 Always use a comma if it is essential to avoid ....

2 Usually use a comma if the support word or set of supporting words comes ....

3 Usually use a comma (brackets or dashes) if ....

4 You may wish to use a comma if the supporting word or set of supporting words comes ....

5 Never use commas if they will .... the reader.

6 When using 'who', make sure that you don't break up the .... by using commas incorrectly. Check by finding the .... group within the **key words**.

8 Trouble Spots

The problems discussed in this chapter are very common in students' writing. Fortunately, they are easy to correct or, better still, avoid. Work through this chapter carefully and then use it as a reference when you are polishing your final draft.

1 Joining and separating sentences

You know that:

- **A sentence must make sense and be complete.**
- **A sentence must contain a subject group and a verb group.**
- **A sentence always contains a set or sets of key words.**
  a The **key words** may form a complete sentence by themselves.

  <u>The lion roared</u>.

  or

  b The sentence may contain a supporting word or set of words.

  Because he was hungry, <u>the lion roared</u>.

  or

  c The sentence may contain more than one set of key words.

  <u>The lion roared</u>, but <u>his mate remained silent</u>.

Trouble Spots

You also know that an essential task of punctuation is to keep your key words apart by a stop stronger than a comma.

> The Mongols attacked India. They were unable to capture Delhi.
>
> (Correct. Separated by a full stop.)
>
> The Mongols attacked India they were unable to capture Delhi.
>
> (Incorrect. **Run-on sentence.**)
>
> The Mongols attacked India, they were unable to capture Delhi.
>
> (Incorrect. **Comma splice.**)
>
> The Mongols attacked India, but were unable to capture Delhi.
>
> (Correct. Separated by a comma plus a joining word.)

When punctuating, you often have a number of options. The one you select will depend upon the precise meaning you wish to convey.

Learn the options and then **you** decide. Choose the one that achieves your purpose. You don't learn punctuation rules; you learn the logic of pauses.

Option one: the full stop

The full stop:

- is the most frequently used stop
- clearly separates sentences
- is the strongest stop
- is generally used, unless the two sentences are closely linked.

For example:

> On Monday Bill cleaned the car. The next day it was involved in an accident.

You Can Write

Option two: the semicolon

Use the semicolon **occasionally** as a substitute for the full stop. It is used to **join** two sentences that are **closely linked**. You use the semicolon when you want to show that the two sets of **key words** are balanced. It creates a pause, but not as strong as the full stop.

> Kick with the other foot; you couldn't be more inaccurate.
> You should be pleased with the team; it has won three games.
> He was a lazy lad; nevertheless, he was always successful.
> ('nevertheless' is a signpost)

The semicolon is particularly useful if you wish to join two closely linked sentences that make a contrast.

> Golf requires a great deal of time; jogging demands hard work.
> Semai women own the houses and fields; Semai men are the priests and leaders of the community.

Do not overuse semicolons. Use them quite deliberately.

Option three: the colon

The colon also joins two sentences.

It is a strong pause but, unlike the full stop, it doesn't indicate an end.

Instead it indicates that what follows is an amplification or explanation of what comes before, and stresses the importance of what comes last. (This is in contrast to the semicolon, where both parts of the sentence are balanced.)

> You should remember one thing: don't fool about with acid.
> The implication is clear: untouchables observe caste customs but not the concepts of pollution and purity.
> Exercise is very healthy: it reduces all kinds of harmful stress.
> Australians have a very bad reputation abroad: they get drunk on every possible occasion.

Option four: the dash

Use very *occasionally* to join two sentences if you wish to create a particularly strong effect. Journalists frequently use dashes.

> Joan refused to marry Tom — she was sick of his irresponsible behaviour.

Option five: the comma plus a joining word

You can join two sentences using a comma *plus* one of the joining words: for, and, nor, but, or, yet, so.

(**Fanboys** helps you remember the joining words: **for and nor but or yet so.** Ray Bailey coined this mnemonic in his *Survival Kit for Writing English*.)
 You have already learnt that you cannot join two sentences with only a comma (comma splice).

> The Mongols attacked India, they were unable to capture Delhi. (Incorrect: Comma splice)

However, a **comma plus** a joining word, such as 'but' (a **fanboys**), is perfectly correct.

> The Mongols attacked India, but they were unable to capture Delhi.

Other examples:

> He left early, for he was not well.
> Punctuation is fun, and it also will improve your grades.
> Mary borrowed the record, but she did not listen to it.
> Wear your jacket, or you will catch cold.
> It was strong, yet it was pleasant.

You will find that many writers, even professionals, omit the comma with a **fanboys**. Only the most fussy marker would penalise you nowadays if you omit the comma. However, you should know which is technically more correct (using the comma) so that you can make up your own mind.

You Can Write

Sometimes, using a comma with a fanboys will result in an unnecessarily clumsy sentence.

Consider the examples I gave above:

Wear a jacket, or you will catch cold.

This is clear and concise. It demonstrates a good use of the comma and **fanboys**.
Now consider this example:

It was strong, yet it was pleasant.

While grammatically correct, this could be condensed:

It was strong yet pleasant.

Again:

Punctuation is fun, and it will also improve your grades.
Besides being fun, punctuation will improve your grades.
You may go to the show, or you may stay at home.
You may go to the show or stay at home.
He was strong, but he was just.
He was strong but just.

To sum up:
Sentences are kept apart by the full stop.

Sentences can be joined by:

- **Semicolon** Used when the sentences are linked very closely, especially if they make a contrast. You use a semicolon to balance two equal sets of key words.
- **Colon** Use a colon if what follows is very closely related to what comes before, especially if the second sentence explains the first. Through the colon you emphasise what comes last.
- **Dash** If you want to be dramatic. Use very selectively.
- **Comma** plus a joining word (**fanboys**). A common way of joining two **complete** sentences.

<u>Underline the **key words** *and punctuate these*.</u> (Don't forget the capital letter after the full stop.) Consider the various options. You'll have a choice in some sentences.

108

Trouble Spots

1 He hunted in the hills and she fished in the streams.
2 She enjoyed sport but he preferred reading.
3 It was strong yet it was pleasant
4 She liked him for a good man is hard to find.
5 Keep your notes brief there is no point in collecting mounds of useless paper.
6 The wives of alcoholics stand by them alcoholic wives are usually deserted by their husbands.
7 Irishmen make excellent husbands they are always kind and understanding.
8 Anthropologists concentrate on the specific sociologists emphasise theories.
9 My objection to the plan is this it will cost a fortune.
10 He had only one thing against her she was utterly ruthless in the way she used people.
11 The school will be closed during vacation but the library will remain open.
12 Frank is my best friend he never lets me down.
13 One system ignores Islam the other emphasises the faith.
14 She loved sports he raved about opera.
15 He was a most objectionable person he swore at the slightest provocation.

Answers:
1 He hunted in the hills, and she fished in the streams.
2 She enjoyed sport, but he preferred reading.
3 It was strong, yet it was pleasant.
4 She liked him, for a good man is hard to find.
5 Keep your notes brief. There is no point in collecting mounds of useless paper.
(or semicolon, colon)
6 The wives of alcoholics stand by them; alcoholic wives are usually deserted by their husbands.
(Semicolon contrasts husbands and wives. Full stop also possible.)
7 Irishmen make excellent husbands: they are always kind and understanding.
(I'd use a colon. It explains why they make excellent husbands. Full stop, dash acceptable.)
8 Anthropologists concentrate on the specific; sociologists emphasise theories.
(or full stop)
9 My objection to the plan is this: it will cost a fortune.
(Colon best. It points forward, emphasising the cost. Full stop, dash acceptable.)

You Can Write

10 He had only one thing against her — she was utterly ruthless in the way she used people.
(A dash for emphasis. Colon next best.)
11 The school will be closed during vacation, but the library will remain open.
12 Frank is my best friend: he never lets me down.
(or full stop, dash)
13 One system ignores Islam; the other emphasises the faith.
(The semicolon points to the contrast.)
14 She loved sports; he raved about the opera.
(or full stop, dash)
15 He was a most objectionable person — he swore at the slightest provocation.
(or take your pick, except the comma)

A *final note*

I hope that you now realise the many options that are open to you. You will rely most heavily on the **full stop**, but don't ignore the alternatives. Punctuate carefully, and your style will be much more expressive.

Now that you have learnt basic punctuation, you should **practise** to gain **confidence**. Get into the habit of studying the punctuation in good quality newspapers, magazines and books. If a 'rule' seems to be broken, study the sentence to see whether it was broken through carelessness or to create a special effect.

2 *Sentence fragment*

Write full sentences, not sentence fragments, except when the particular form of writing requires otherwise. Make sure that the sentence has a **subject group** and **verb** group. The sentence must be **complete**.

> *Sentence fragments*:
> On the way to work.
> Although he works hard.
> When the discovery had been made and the news of it had reached to scientists.

Words ending in 'ing' are often found in sentence fragments.

> Each one *having* a different effect on steel.
> This *being* the introduction of missiles.

110

Words like 'having' and 'being' are not complete verbs. They need a part of the verb 'to be', e.g. was having, is being, before they can take a subject. This is correct:

> Each one *was having* a different effect on steel.

This error often occurs in a long sentence fragment.

3 Comma splice

You can't join sentences with a comma.

These are incorrect:

> Aristotle was a famous philosopher, he influenced most later Western philosophers.
> Edison seemed to be interested in everything, he experimented in the field of medicine and developed a programme for farm relief.

The comma splice error is extremely common, not only in student essays, but also in newspapers and magazines.

The comma splice error often occurs when a signpost word comes at the start of the second statement.

This is incorrect:

> Plato was a famous philosopher, however, his influence waned for many centuries. (**Key words** underlined.)

Some students assume that signpost words act as joining words (**fanboys**). They don't!

While signpost words may seem to act like **fanboys**, their role is much more restricted: they are *not* joining words.

If in doubt:

- Check to see if it is a fanboys (for, and, nor, but, or, yet, so).
- If not, remove the signpost and check for a comma splice.

Common signpost words: however, therefore, nevertheless, consequently, moreover, for example, on the other hand.

> The essay was late, consequently, the student lost marks.

Remove 'consequently'. Error: Comma splice.

You Can Write

4 Run-on sentence

This error is very similar to the **comma splice**, except that the comma is omitted altogether.
Incorrect:

> Aristotle was a famous philosopher he influenced most later Western philosophers.
> During this time, Edison was working on many telegraphic improvements some of his inventions included receivers, automatic printers and tapes.
> (This requires a full stop after 'improvements'.)

A signpost word at the start of the sentence does not let you break this rule. Use the same check as you used for the comma splice: remove the signpost.

> Plato was a famous philospher however, his influence waned for many centuries.

This is still a **run-on sentence**. (A full stop or a semi-colon is required after philosopher.)

5 Apostrophe

The apostrophe is used:
- **To indicate that a letter has been omitted from a word. The word has been shortened.**

was not	—	wasn't
do not	—	don't
is not	—	isn't
we are	—	we're
they are	—	they're
it is	—	it's

- **To indicate that somebody or something owns something. The owner takes the apostrophe.**

An easy way to make sure you are correct is to:
- **write down who or what is the owner** (Don't add an apostrophe simply because a word ends with 's'.)

Trouble Spots

- **write down who or what is actually owned**
- **put in the apostrophe**
- **sound the word to see if an 's' is needed**.

    Johns hat (the hat of **John**)
    John
    John'
    John's hat (Obviously an 's' is needed. The sound of the word tells you. You don't say 'John hat'.)

The apostrophe tells you that the part of the word that comes before it is the owner:

    Tom's head   — Tom
    a baby's head   — baby
    the babies' heads   — babies
    the dogs' heads   — dogs

Some examples:

    the childrens toys (the toys of the **children**)
    children
    children'
    the children's toys
    the ladies husbands (the husbands of the **ladies**)
    ladies
    ladies'
    the ladies' husbands (no extra 's' needed)
    a ladys name (the name of a **lady**)
    lady
    lady'
    a lady's name
    Charles crown (the crown of **Charles**)
    Charles
    Charles'
    Charles's crown (the sound tells you)
    the witches sabbath (the sabbath of the **witches**)
    witches
    witches'
    the witches' sabbath (no 's' needed)

You Can Write

If you come across a really unusual example, you may simply wish to rephrase (rewrite):

> My sons-in-law's boat sank. Not sure? Then: The boat belonging to my sons-in-law sank.

However, apostrophes are very useful and easy to use, so don't be scared of them.

Many students who don't know how to use the apostrophe correctly stick them in blindly whenever they see an 's' at the end of a word.

For example:
> The ladies' saw Tess' in Las' Vegas'.
Don't do it: It's wrong. There must be possession!

Try these:

1 a mans name
2 a books cover
3 the books titles
4 a boys nose
5 Marxs theory
6 Gandhis movement
7 The hostesss face
8 the authors addiction
9 Ones emotional reaction
10 Freuds pan-sexualism

Answers:
1 man's 2 book's 3 books' (more than one) 4 boy's 5 Marx's 6 Gandhi's 7 hostess's 8 author's if one author; authors' if more than one. 9 one's 10 Freud's.

6 *Use of it's*

It's is only used for it is. The apostrophe in 'it's' indicates that a letter (i) has been left out and that the word has been shortened.

When you use it's, substitute in your mind 'it is'. If it makes sense, then you are correct.

> It's a boy. (Correct)
> He knew it's name. (Incorrect)

Try these:

1 He heard that it's correct.
2 He realised it's significance.
3 He saw its' relevance.
4 The car landed on its back.
5 How can you be sure that it's not still burning?

Answers:
1 Correct   2 Incorrect   3 Incorrect   4 Correct   5 Correct

7 *Question mark*

Always use a question mark when you ask a direct question or quote someone else's direct question. Do not use a question mark if the question is not direct.

> Given these facts, can one make a prediction? (direct question)
> He asked, 'Who started the riot?'. (direct question, quoted)
> He demanded to know who killed the man. (indirect question)

8 *Semicolon*

Use the semicolon to separate the items in a complex list. (Normally you would use commas.)

> He needed the following items: a long, strong piece of rope; a toy horse and cart; a rocket, including the launching pad; and a Santa Claus outfit.

If you use only commas, the list is confusing — a long, strong piece of rope, a toy horse and cart, a rocket, including this launching pad, and a Santa Claus outfit.

9 *The colon*

Use the colon to announce something.
A list:

> My fishing boat contains everything: tackle, spare lines, lifejackets and plenty of cold drinks.

115

You Can Write

> The weight of a body depends upon two factors: its mass and its distance from the centre of the earth.

A direct question:

> People continually ask me this: 'Of what possible use are the Social Sciences?'

10 Exclamation mark

Use very, very occasionally to add emphasis.

> The silence was deafening!

11 I or me? we or us? they or them?

When there are no intervening words, it is easy:

> *I* am ill.
> He laughed at *me*
> He asked *us* home.
> *We* shall be glad to work overtime.

The trouble arises when words are inserted:

> He laughed at Tom and (I/me).
> (We/us) girls shall be glad to work overtime.
> (They/them) and the partners are discussing the court proceedings.

Solution? Remove (in your mind) the extra words.
You can even bracket them if you wish.

> He hit Tom and me. (He hit . . . me.)
> We girls shall be glad to work overtime. (We . . . shall)
> They and the partners are discussing the court proceedings. (They are . . . discussing)

Add (in your mind) the verb:

> She is taller than (I/me).
> She is taller than *I*. (am)
> You are as bright as (he/him).
> You are as bright as *he*. (is)

Try these. (Either mentally omit intervening words or add a verb.)

1 Mrs Jones invited her and (I/me) to the dance.
2 Sam and (I/me) will carry out the extensions.
3 Between her and (I/me), an understanding grew.
4 They sent it to Fred and (he/him).
5 (We/us) students would rather play than work.
6 She is quicker than (I/me).
7 They love you as much as (I/me).
8 We are stronger than (they/them).

Answers:
1 Mrs Jones invited . . . *me*
2 *I* will
3 Between . . . *me*
4 . . . sent . . . to . . . *him*
5 *We* . . . would
6 . . . than *I* (am).
7 They love . . . *me*
8 . . . than *they* (are)

12 Subject/verb agreement

If the **subject** is **singular** (refers to one only), then the verb must be **singular**. If the **subject** is **plural** (refers to more than one), then the **verb** must be **plural**. Agreement means that both the subject and verb must be plural, or both must be singular.

> The boys (plural subject) play (plural verb) in the street.
> (Correct)
> The boys (plural subject) play (plural verb) in the street.
> (Incorrect)
> Tom and Mary (plural subject) plays (singular verb) in the street.
> (Incorrect)

Usually this presents no problem, except:

- When the **subject** is **separated** from the **verb**:

> The effective use of these computers (requires/require) detailed study.
> (subject: use   verb: requires)

117

You Can Write

> The behaviour of these people (is/are) disgusting. (subject: behaviour   verb: is)
> A roster of all staff members (is/are) being compiled. (subject: roster   verb: is)
> Another major feature of the Martian landscape (is/are) the massive volcano mountains found in the Tharsis region. (subject: feature   verb: is)

- With such words as **each**, **every**, **either**, **neither**, **anyone**, **everyone**, **no one**, **somebody**, **nobody**. They are all **singular**. The *one* is the clue. 'One' is singular. Each (one), every (one), neither (one).

> Each (is/are) ill.
> Each (one) *is* ill.
> Each of the boys (is/are) ill.
> Each (one) of the boys *is* ill.
> Neither (has/have) any money.
> Neither (one) *has* any money.
> Neither Bill nor Tom (has/have) any money.
> Neither (one) Bill nor Tom *has* any money.

- With collective nouns. A collective noun is the name given to a number of individuals which, together, constitute a group.

For example:

> Crowd, audience, government, mob, political party.

Use singular or plural, depending on the meaning.

Singular when they remain one (a unit):

> The crowd applauds enthusiastically.

Plural when they are divided (the unity is broken):

> The mob are fighting among themselves.
> (They are no longer a unit.)

> The audience was delighted with her dancing.
> (They are united.)

> The audience were divided in *their* opinions.
> (They are divided.)

Trouble Spots

Try these. Use reason not rules.

1 The boy, as well as some other criminals, (was/were) sent to Australia.
2 The risk of further explosions (is/are) great. (subject: the risk).
3 None of the poeple (was/were) interested in his story.
4 Everyone has (his or her/their) own story.
5 The reason for the riots (was/were) the poor working conditions.
6 Neither of the boys (is/are) well.
7 The crowd (was/were) divided over the merits of his performance.
8 The government (is/are) happy with the budget.
9 The list of all the late arrivals (is/are) being sent to the lecturer.

Answers:
1 was (subject: boy)   2 is   3 was (not *one* was)   4 his or her   5 was (subject: reason)   6 is (neither one)   7 were (collective noun 'crowd' — plural, as they were not united)   8 is   9 is

13 Parallelism

Make sure that you maintain a regular pattern when writing a series of things. Compare these pairs of sentences:

> Jogging is pleasant, inexpensive, and it helps you lose weight. (Notice how the pattern is broken. It distracts and irritates the reader.)
> Jogging is pleasant, inexpensive and helps you lose weight.

> She was an excellent technician and could also repair cars.
> She was an excellent technician and mechanic.

> Study develops the mind; exercise develops the body; but the heart is only developed by life.
> Study develops the mind: exercise develops the body; but only life develops the heart.

> Silica is placed on the inside of the light globe to scatter light from the filament and it also reduces glare.
> Silica is placed on the inside of the light globe to scatter light from the filament and also to reduce glare.

119

You Can Write

14 Danglers — *faulty reference*

Running to catch a train, the purse was dropped by Mary.

This reads as if the purse were doing the running. The words 'running to catch the train' are dangling or hanging uncomfortably. You don't know whether they refer to the 'purse' or to 'Mary'. To whom do they refer?

So rewrite:

Running to catch a train, Mary dropped her purse.

Again:

Then, speaking hesitantly and emotionally, a single tear ran down his nose. (From the *Weekend Australian*, 22–23 Sept., 1984)

Then, while he was speaking hesitantly and emotionally, a single tear ran down his nose.

Rewrite to eliminate danglers:

1 Bowing to the crowd, the bull caught him by surprise.

2 Constructed of rough stones and straw roofs, the peasants find that their houses are comfortable.

3 When entering the room, the books fell on him.

4 By keeping national parks, the earth will be a much healthier place.

5 Going home, I found the path slippery.

6 The forecourt is an eyecatching and exciting sight when rushing through the traffic.

7 Having dented the bonnet, he drove the car carefully.

8 Having already been dented on the bonnet, he drove the car carefully.

....

9 Walking down the street, the rain started to pour.

....

Some possibilities:

1 When the matador bowed to the crowd, the bull caught him by surprise.
2 Although the houses are constructed of rough stones and straw roofs, the peasants find them comfortable.
3 As he entered the room, the books fell on him.
4 If we keep (or preserve) national parks, the earth will be a much healthier place.
5 Correct.
6 When one is rushing through the traffic, the forecourt is an eyecatching and exciting sight.
7 Correct.
8 Having already dented the bonnet, he drove the car carefully.
9 As I was walking down the street, the rain started to pour.

15 Poor spelling

Although you will find examples of incorrect spelling in all sorts of strange places (newspapers, school reports, advertisements), it is still extremely important that you spell correctly. You can't expect your reader to take your written work seriously if you don't bother to use a dictionary. Bad spelling suggests that you are careless, illiterate and lazy. I know that this is often unfair, but this is the impression poor spelling conveys.

What options are open to you if you are a poor speller?

- Ignore the problem and hope that your reader will also ignore it or will forgive you. Frankly, I don't fancy your chances.
- Hire a typist or proofreader who has a good command of English.
- Buy a word processor with a spelling program.
- Improve your spelling.

You Can Write

If you want to improve your spelling, here are a few suggestions:

- Learn to use a dictionary correctly; many adults have not. Try to get hold of a school text that teaches dictionary skills. You will find that most dictionaries have a guide to their use. This guide, which usually appears at the beginning of the dictionary, will explain the format for definitions, the rules about foreign words and phrases, the pronunciation guide, and so on.
- Keep a dictionary on your desk at all times. Get into the habit of using it.
- Keep a list of words that you frequently misspell.
- Concentrate on words. Study them carefully. Say them clearly.
- Don't check every word while you are writing, as that interrupts your train of thought. Check them when you are revising and giving the final polish to your piece.
- Consider using one of the many excellent spelling aids available in kit form or on computer tapes.
- Develop confidence. You *will* eventually learn.
- Get help with your proofreading.
- Some texts set out a list of spelling rules. Frankly, I have found them a waste of time, as there are so many exceptions, but you may find them useful.

Remember the Chinese saying: 'The longest journey begins with a single step'. You will get there in the end.

Final review

Punctuate and correct grammar where necessary. Some sentences are correct. Underline **key words** *if you have any doubts.*

1 These goods for example were sold in Toms house.
2 Facts by themselves are not science but science deals with facts.
3 History examines the specific sociology is concerned about theory.

Trouble Spots

4 The protozoa which live in a symbiotic relationship within the stomach of a termite actually digest the woody material.
5 History examines the specific, sociology on the other hand is about theory.
6 The test puzzles I but neither of the girls were fooled.
7 If you are late you will not have time to finish the test.
8 Some of these remains are of species we know today others like Diprotodon are known only from the past.
9 People who falsify their tax returns should be fined heavily.
(Only those who falsify their tax returns.)
10 I shall only support a football team that is coached by Barry Cable. (You'll only follow Cable's team.)
11 One of the boxes are missing and its the ladys fault.
12 He had only one complaint the service was disgusting.
13 After the fight was over the two men shook hands.
14 Gerontologists divide the problems of the aged into three categories medical financial and social.
15 Migrants who have a criminal record should be deported.
(Only those with a record should be deported.)
16 The comma splice is a common error for instance it is becoming increasingly common in student essays.
17 It was discovered that English sailors who were fond of the juices of lemons or limes did not succumb to scurvy.
18 Albinism lack of all pigmentation is a mutation that appears in plants mice rats rabbits and birds as well as human beings.
19 The human body consists of about 60 per cent water in fact the water contains the same salts that are dissolved in ocean water.
20 Note this final point do not feel that you must satisfy everybody.

Answers:

1 These goods, for example, <u>were sold in Tom's house</u>.
2 <u>Facts by themselves are not science</u>, but <u>science deals with facts</u>.
3 <u>History examines the specific; sociology is concerned about theory</u>.
(or full stop)

You Can Write

4 <u>The protozoa</u>, which live in a symbiotic relationship within the stomach of a termite, actually digest the woody material.
5 History examines the <u>specific</u>; <u>sociology</u>, on the other hand, <u>is about theory</u>.
  (or full stop — note signpost 'on the other hand')
6 The test puzzles me, but neither of the girls was fooled.
7 If you are late, <u>you will not have time to finish the test.</u>
8 Some of these remains are of species we know today; <u>others</u>, like Diprotodon, are known only from the past.
9 People who <u>falsify their tax returns should be fined heavily.</u>
10 I shall only support a football team that is coached by <u>Barry Cable.</u>
11 <u>One of the boxes is missing, and it's the lady's fault.</u>
  (or full stop, colon, semicolon)
12 He had only one complaint — the service was disgusting.
13 After the fight was over, <u>the two men shook hands.</u>
14 Gerontologists divide the problems of the aged into three categories: <u>medical, financial and social.</u>
  (colon introducing a list)
15 Migrants who have a criminal record should be deported.
16 <u>The comma splice is a common error; for instance, it is becoming</u> increasingly common in many student essays.
  (or full stop — note signpost)
17 <u>It was discovered that English sailors who were fond of the juices of lemons or limes did not succumb to scurvy.</u>
18 <u>Albinism, lack of all pigmentation, is a mutation that appears in plants, mice, rats, rabbits and birds, as well as human beings.</u>
  (or brackets or dashes)
19 The human body consists of about 60 per cent water. In fact, <u>the water contains the same salts that are dissolved in ocean water.</u>
  (or semicolon after water — note the signpost)
20 Note this final point: <u>do not feel that you must satisfy everybody.</u>
  (colon emphasising the second part of the sentence)

9 Referencing Skills

In 'Planning your essay' (chapter 3) and 'Book reviews' (chapter 10), I discuss basic research skills: how to find books, journal articles and book reviews. The other important skill you need is the ability to **reference** correctly.

What follows may seem complicated, but really is not difficult. Take it easily. Most of it is commonsense. Study the examples and practise: it will fall into place.

A major difference between school and tertiary essays (and reports) is that the latter requires thorough referencing.

Most inexperienced tertiary students find referencing a complex and worrying business; even many experienced students are unable to reference accurately, confidently or intelligently. Yet, once the basic skills are learnt, referencing becomes a largely mechanical exercise. Moreover, thorough and accurate referencing gives an essay a professional, polished appearance (so long as you don't simply list references to try to fool the lecturer into believing that you have read more than you actually have). Good referencing can often mean the difference between a good and an average mark.

Why reference?

Referencing is an essential component of the essay or report. You reference in order to show the reader what evidence you have collected to support your argument.

The most pressing reason for referencing is that you will probably lose marks for your essay or report if you don't. You might get away with it for a while, but eventually you will be penalised. Learn how to reference now and you won't be placed in that embarrassing position.

You Can Write

What is referencing?

Referencing is the method of acknowledging sources of information and ideas within the essay or report that are not your own. Obviously, at the undergraduate level, you will obtain most of your facts, theories and ideas from other sources, mainly books and articles, and so you must learn how to reference them accurately and thoroughly.

What do you reference?

- Any fact that a reasonably well-read person would not be expected to know. For example, you would not reference the fact that the First World War broke out in 1914 or that Sir John Kerr dismissed the Whitlam Government in 1975 or that Dublin is the capital city of Ireland. Referencing is largely a matter of commonsense; don't work yourself up worrying whether you have referenced every single fact.
- Another person's ideas, theories or distinctive writing style.
- Statistical material, maps, diagrams.
- Direct quotations from your sources.

This seems a lot, but once you have mastered the basic skills and have had some practice, referencing becomes almost automatic.

How do you reference?

Every discipline has a slightly different system and, fortunately, usually publishes guides to those systems. Find out which system is used in the department to which you will submit your essay or report. (You may even find that lecturers within the same department will insist that you use different systems, but that's an aspect of academic life that you'll just have to live with.) However, most lecturers in the Sciences and Social Sciences accept the **Harvard System** (developed at Harvard University) or a version of that system. Once you have learnt one system, you can easily adapt it if need be; referencing principles are always the same. I'll use the Harvard System as an example.

When referencing you must be:
- **Accurate**: the details must be correct
- **Consistent**: use the same system in the same way throughout.
- **Thorough**: give *all* the required information.

Step one: take down full bibliographical details and the page number when taking notes for your essay

Referencing actually begins at the notetaking stage.

- Record the bibliographical details of the book or article when you start to take notes.
  (I'll demonstrate later how to find these details.)
- Record the page numbers while you are taking notes.

Step two: referencing in the body of your essay

For example:

> The height of most humans falls within a fairly limited range. However, a few extremely tall and very short individuals are found. Many of these have abnormal growths in the anterior pituitary gland (Davidson 1982: 28).

The shorthand very quickly provides the reader with the following information:

Davidson	=	the name of the person who wrote the book or article.
1982	=	the year in which the book or article was published.
:	=	a shorthand way of writing page or pages.
28	=	the page in Davidson's work where the information can be found.

The reader now knows that the information you've given about a possible cause of extreme tallness or shortness in humans can be found on page 28 in Davidson's book or article published in 1982. The reader can turn to the reference list, which is at the back of the essay, to find full details of the book or article — see Step Three below.

Note: Always provide the page numbers when referencing. The only exception is when you are making a very general reference to a work.

For example:

> One of the most important contributions to the theory of suicide has been made by Emile Durkheim (1952). (The entire book, entitled *Suicide: A Study in Sociology* is about suicide. Putting Durkheim (1952: 1–999) would look silly.)

However, when you are being at all specific, you must give the page number:

> Durkheim (1952: 158) argues that Protestants are more likely to commit suicide than Catholics and Jews because . . .

Step three: provide a reference list (or bibliography) at the end of your essay

The reference list is a list of the books, articles and other materials that are mentioned or referred to in the text of your essay. (A bibliography is all of these as well as any other material that you may have read but have not specifically mentioned or referred to. Historians, who like their students to read widely, usually like a bibliography, but most are satisfied with a reference list. Make up your own mind, unless instructed otherwise.)

In the reference list (or bibliography) you would, for example, list the book by Davidson that you mentioned in the text.

For example:

Reference List

Abrahams, David
1984   <u>An Introduction to Biology</u>. Bombay: Oxford University Press.

Referencing Skills

Davidson, Alan John
1982   <u>Biological Science</u>. London: John Brown Publishers.
Smith, P.
1985   <u>Biology Made Simple: An Introductory Text for Secondary Students</u>. London: Heinemann.

You can find all these details on the title page inside of the book and in the page on the back of the title page.

Set out your reference list (or bibliography) in alphabetical order by the authors' surnames.

Provide:

1 The author's surname.
2 The author's given name or names as they appear on the title (inside) page of the book. Don't give only initials if the title page gives the author's given name.
3 The date of publication (when the book was published).
4 The *full* title of the book as it appears on the title page.
5 The place of publication — give the city (Bombay) not the country (India).
6 The publisher.

(This information enables your reader to locate Davidson's book quickly and check your facts.)

Remember: steps in referencing

- **Step one: when making notes, take down the page number and full bibliographical details: author, title, date of publication, place of publication and publisher.** (You'll need these for your reference list or bibliography.)
- **Step two: insert the reference at the appropriate place within the essay.** You can use the Harvard System or one of the numbering systems.
- **Step three: provide a reference list** (or bibliography) **at the end of your essay.**

Once you know these three steps, you know the basis of referencing. If you have any doubts, go back over what you have just read. Now let's consider some further points

129

Finding bibliographical details from a book

You can find these bibliographical details in the title page inside the book and in the page on the back of the title page.

For example:

Title page

A Guide to Learning Independently
Lorraine A. Marshall
Frances Rowland
Murdoch University

Longman Cheshire

Imprint page

Longman Cheshire Pty Limited
95 Coventry Street
Melbourne 3205 Australia

Offices in Sydney, Brisbane, Adelaide and Perth.
Associated companies, branches, and representatives throughout the world

© Longman Cheshire Pty Ltd 1981

First published 1981
Reprinted 1983, 1984, 1985

We can easily set this out correctly. The only problem is the date of publication — is it 1981 or 1983?

The word reprinted (or impression) simply means that the book has been popular and the publisher has run off (printed) more copies without changes. Ignore all references to printings or impressions.

Now set out the bibliographical details:

Now check your setting out:

  Marshall, Lorraine A. & Rowland, Frances
  1981 A Guide to Learning Independently. Melbourne:
      Longman Cheshire.

Note:

- the authors' full names.
- the title underlined.
- the city (Melbourne) not Australia.

Sometimes the book will be a new or revised edition. This will be indicated by the words 'Second Edition' or 'Revised Edition' or 'Third (revised) Edition'. These words may appear underneath the title:

The Practical Stylist
  Fourth Edition
    or

on the next page:

First edition 1952
Second edition 1955
Reprinted 1957
Third edition 1964

You Can Write

A new or revised edition means that changes have been made to the text, and usually means that the page numbers also have been changed. You must tell the reader what edition you are using so that she or he can check accurately.

Let's take another example:

The Spirit and Purpose of Geography

S.W. Wooldridge
late Professor of Geography in the
University of London
&
W.G. East
Professor of Geography in the
University of London

**Hutchinson University Library
London**

No problems. Ignore the titles (professor) of the authors.

Wooldridge, S.W. and East W.G.
　　　　The Spirit and Purpose of Geography. London:
　　　　Hutchinson University Library.

Referencing Skills

You still need the publication date. Turn over the page of the book. You'll find:

> HUTCHINSON & CO (Publishers) Ltd
> 178–202 Great Portland Street, London W1
>
> London Melbourne Sydney
> Auckland Bombay Toronto
> Johannesburg New York
>
> *
>
> First published 1951
> Reprinted 1952, 1955, 1956
> Second (revised) edition 1958
> Reprinted 1960, 1962, 1963, 1964
> Third (revised) edition 1966
>
> © S.W. Wooldridge and W.G. East 1951, 1958, 1966.

Confusing? Go back to what I said. You need to find the latest date when the book was **revised**, that is when a **new edition** appeared. Remember, you ignore reprinting.

So: the third (revised) edition was 1966. That is the publication date.

Therefore:

Wooldridge, S.W. and East, W.G.
1966   The Spirit and Purpose of Geography. 3rd ed.
          London: Hutchinson University Library.

Notice we put in 3rd ed. (third edition) to make absolutely sure. Don't bother to note an edition number if it is the first edition. Remember also to note only the first place mentioned. Ignore Melbourne, Sydney, etc.

Try this:

> © S. Encel 1970
> First published 1970
> Reprinted 1972
> by F.W. Cheshire Publishing Pty Ltd
> 346 St. Kilda Road, Melbourne
> Also at Sydney, Adelaide and Brisbane

Published? ....

133

Publisher? ....
Where published? ....
Think. *Don't write your answer unless you are sure.*
        Published: 1970. (We ignore reprinted. Remember?)
        Publisher: Cheshire. (We don't bother with F. W. or Publishing Pty Ltd. They're not incorrect, just unnecessary.)
        Where published: Melbourne. (Remember: the first city mentioned.)

Sometimes the bibliographical details are very complicated. Government publications are particularly tricky. If you are not sure, you should check the entry in the library's catalogue.

For example:

A typical catalogue card

378.1702812
        MARSHALL, LORRAINE A.
A guide to learning independently / Lorraine A. Marshall, Frances Rowland– – Melbourne : Longman Cheshire, 1981 – – 224p.

While the catalogue entry may contain some information that you don't require, you should use it if you are not sure. For example, note the publication date (1981), which caused us some concern above.

    (Note: Never rely on reading lists to obtain bibliographical details: they are notoriously inaccurate.)

Finding bibliographical details from a journal article

You need to copy down the details from the journal, as the catalogue cards will not help. Fortunately, finding the correct bibliographical details from a journal presents no problems once you've had some practice.
For example:

Title page

>Journal of
>FAMILY ISSUES
>
>Volume 2 Number 1   March 1981
>
>   CONTENTS
>
>Notes from the Editor's Desk
> GRAHAM B. SPANIER   3
>
>Attitudes Toward Reproductive Engineering: an Overview
> SHIRLEY FOSTER HARTLEY   5
>
>Protective Labor Legislation and the Cult of Domesticity
> AVA BARON   25
>
>The Well-being of Persons Remarried after Divorce
> NORVAL D. GLENN   61
>
>Divorce and Suicide: a Time Series Analysis, 1933–1970
> STEVEN STACK   77

Set out Glenn's article like this:

>Glenn, Norval D.
>1981   'The well-being of persons remarried after divorce', *Journal of Family Issues*, 2,1 (March): 61–76.

Notice the punctuation. **Be consistent**. (You can, however, either follow the capitalisation of the title as printed, or use only small letters.)

Use the contents page of the journal to check the following:

1 the author's surname
2 the author's given name(s) — not initials if possible

3 the date of publication
4 the title of the actual article — in inverted commas
5 the title of the journal — underline it
6 the volume number (2) — journals usually begin a new volume each year
7 the issue number (1) — a journal usually publishes a number of issues or parts during the year
8 the month (March) or season (e.g. Summer) in which the journal came out
9 the actual pages in the journal where the article can be found. (An article may end a page or two before the next begins.)

This seems a lot, but it makes sense. You are providing your reader with plenty of information so that she or he can go to the library, find the issue of the journal (there may be hundreds of issues in a particular journal), open the journal and immediately find the article to which you have referred. You, of course, can do the same when you are using published materials for your own research.

Now set out Blakeney's article in the following:

THE SYDNEY LAW REVIEW	
Volume 9, No. 1 January, 1980	
The Anatomy of an Administrative Decision, The Hon. Mr. Justice Brennan	1
Buyer Liability Under Section 49 of the Trade Practices Act 1974, Michael Blakeney	27
The Contract of Employment and Freedom of Speech, G.J. McCarry	33

Now check:

Blakeney, Michael
1980   'Buyer Liability Under Section 49 of the Trade Practices Act 1974', *The Sydney Law Review*, 9, 1 (January): 27–32.

Variations in referencing

You can set out your reference in different ways depending upon your — or your lecturer's — preference or upon the kind of material you are using.

- The reference can be placed at the end of the sentence or sentences to which it refers.

  For example:

  > Because of usurious interest rates, a tribal is sometimes forced to resort to the Khandagutta arrangement; that is, giving his creditor the use of his land in lieu of interest. Once this has occurred, the tribal has little chance of redeeming his land (Brown 1977: 48–64).

  The reader now knows that material in these two sentences is taken from pages 48 to 64 of the book Brown published in 1977.

- The reference can be placed close to the beginning of the material. You should do this if all of a long paragraph is taken from the same reference; otherwise the reader won't know whether the whole paragraph or just the last sentence is taken from the source. The reader might assume that the first part is yours.

  For example:

  > According to Smith (1981: 22), alienation occurs most frequently among women who belong to the lower socio-economic level of society. They have not the means to escape from their restrictive environments, and thus suffer from a wide range of psychological disorders. To support her argument, Smith uses the evidence from her study of 280 women living in a poorer part of Melbourne, where she found that over 25 per cent of women had taken tranquillising drugs regularly over a twelve-month period (Smith 1981: 24).

Referencing is not an exact science: there are no precise rules about when and how you reference. You have some choice, but be thorough, accurate and consistent. It is best to be overconscientious at first, so long as you don't become obsessive.

Direct Quotations

Direct quotations are words (sometimes a few words, sometimes a long passage) copied directly from a book, article or some other source.

Use them sparingly. Their value is in what use you make of them, not in their simply existing. Never submit an essay that consists largely of direct quotations. This strategy is sometimes used, as a last resort, by very desperate students, but it doesn't work.

Use direct quotations for a specific purpose, such as:

- to summarise a crucial argument or key point:

    According to Andreski (1972: 80), role theory consists of 'pompous, nebulous and incredibly lengthy restatements of what has been common knowledge for a very long time'.

    As Moore (1973: 410) states, 'the poor bear the heaviest costs of modernisation under both socialist and capitalist auspices'.

- to provide an exact definition:

    According to Geertz (1960: 6), the term *prijaji* 'originally referred only to the hereditary aristocracy which the Dutch pried loose from the kings of the vanquished native states and turned into an appointive, salaried civil service'.

- to use a particularly catchy expression or phrase:

    For instance, Wilson (1954: 15) described the 'startling and significant success' of the . . .

(The repetition of the s's obviously appealed to the writer.) Bear in mind, however, that in most cases you should paraphrase; that is, write in your own words.

Guidelines for using direct quotations:
- **Keep them short.**
- **Use them sparingly.**
- **Use them for a specific reason.**
- **Reproduce them exactly — word for word — including spelling or grammatical errors.** (See 'Errors in the original' at the end of this chapter.)

- **Reference them accurately.**
- **Set them out consistently.**

Setting-out direct quotations

1 Short quotations

Most of your quotations will be short (see above); less than twenty words.

Short quotations are set out within the text. You can set your reference out in different ways, provided that it is clear to what you are referring.

- *Reference at the end of the quotation*:
  For example:

    Rich peasants have no compunction about taking on the role previously held by the non-tribal moneylenders, and 'do not hesitate to exploit their own people' (Bose 1981: 191). In many parts of India, however, urban merchants are the chief source of credit.

- *Reference before the quotation*:
  For example:

    Gould (1971: 145) even asserts that it is 'the most undependable and impoverished environment anywhere in the world where people have succeeded in living off the land'.

2 Long quotations

As a rough guide, a long quotation is more than one sentence, or more than five lines.

The long quotation is:

- indented (no quotation marks)
- introduced by the colon (:)
- single-spaced.

The reference can come after the author's name.
For example:

    In discussing the nature of gases, Hess (1971: 60) provides a comprehensive definition of matter:

> Matter exists in three physical states: gaseous, liquid, and solid. A gas has no internal boundary. It expands to fill any container completely, regardless of the size or shape of the container. A liquid has one internal boundary, its surface. A solid is rigid, that is, it bounds itself internally in all dimensions.

Hess then goes on to discuss further how each of the states of matter differ. He states that ...
>> or
... that is, it bounds itself internally in all dimensions (Hess 1971: 60).
(Note the position of the fullstop, which 'ties' the reference into the quotation.)

Plagiarism: the mortal sin

Most course outlines warn you against plagiarism. Some threaten dire punishments if you are caught.

- **Plagiarism will occur if you omit references — your writing will suggest that the facts or ideas are yours when, in fact, you have read them elsewhere.**
- **Plagiarism is presenting someone else's work as your own.**
- **Plagiarism is a kind of stealing.**
- **Plagiarism may involve the use of a phrase, a sentence, a paragraph, an idea.**
- **Plagiarism is sometimes deliberate, but most first-year students plagiarise by accident.**
- **Copying another student's essay is not plagiarism: it's cheating.**

Take some examples:

Original:

> 'No living being can be happy or even exist unless his needs are sufficiently proportioned to his means' (Durkheim 1952: 215).

Plagiarism in order of severity:

> No living being can be happy or even exist unless his needs are sufficiently proportioned to his means.

(No mention of source — straightforward stealing.)
Durkheim (1952: 215) argues that no living being can be happy or even exist unless his needs are sufficiently proportioned to his means.
(Copied directly. No quotation marks. Still plagiarism.)
No being can be satisfied or even survive unless his needs are proportioned to his means (Durkheim 1952: 215).
(This is still plagiarism, even though a reference is provided. You've only made a few minor changes. This form of plagiarism is more often a result of careless or poor technique than deliberate cheating.)

Take another example:

Original:

'In the Far West, barbarian war bands and migrating hordes broke into the Roman Empire; similar, though less numerous, hordes invaded north China. In both areas, the invaders set up short-lived states and gradually acquired some of the culture of their subjects' (McNeill: 1963: 362).

Plagiarised version:

According to McNeill (1963: 362), war bands of barbarians and hordes of migrants attacked the Roman Empire. The hordes that attacked north China were less numerous. In Rome and in China the invaders set up a series of ephemeral states and, in time, adopted some of the culture of the people they had conquered.
(The writer implies that the only information he or she got from McNeill was that in the first sentence. Note how closely the student has paraphrased.)

A correct version:

According to McNeill (1963: 362), both the Roman Empire and, to a lesser extent, north China were overrun by barbarian tribes. These founded states that did not survive for very long. They also became partly civilised through contact with their subjects. (McNeill 1963: 363).
(This is not so well written, but is much more acceptable.)

141

You Can Write

How to avoid plagiarism

If you put into practice the suggestions made in this book, you will have no worries. It is virtually impossible to avoid some unconscious plagiarism when you are writing your first research papers. Lecturers realise this, and so long as you make a sincere effort and follow the guidelines below, you will not be severely penalised. However, it's not worth running the risk of deliberately plagiarising, especially as you will be rewarded for acknowledging sources and referencing properly.

Guidelines
- **Be honest.**
- **Reference fully.**
- **Develop paraphrasing skills.** Rewrite in your own words.
- **Take careful notes.**
- **Plan your essay.**

Direct quotations: further examples

Using a quotation that is quoted in a book or article.
Sometimes you may wish to use a quotation that the author of the book has himself quoted.
For example:

> Brown (as quoted by Smith 1980: 40) argues that 'capitalism is deader than the dodo'.

Your reference list or bibliography will, of course, list Smith's book.
   These are further technical points. (Don't try to memorise them. Refer to them when you need to do so.)

1 Errors in the original

You must reproduce the original exactly. In order to show that the error is not yours, use [sic] meaning 'thus' (as it was in the original). Use square brackets [ ] to enclose 'sic'.
For example:

> 'The cases of suicize [sic] are too numerous to discuss in detail.'

2 Emphasis

You may wish to emphasise a word or section within a quotation.
For example:

'An Irishman's weakness is <u>alcohol</u> not sex' (emphasis added).

This tells the reader that you have underlined.
If the emphasis is in the original, you may, if you wish, add (emphasis in the original).

3 Ellipsis

You may omit a word, phrase or sentence from the quotation. Use . . . or . . . . if the material left out includes a fullstop or fullstops.

Moore (1973: 31) discussed the repression in Europe that followed the outbreak of revolution in France. He argues:

> The outbreak of the French Revolution put an end to all hope of reform . . . . England began to enter a phase of repression that lasted until after the Napoleonic Wars. Its fundamental fortune was that the upper classes . . . closed ranks around patriotic and conservative slogans against the menace of radicalism and tyranny in France and against the remotest threat to their privileges.

(I omitted an entire sentence in the first section and part of a sentence later.)

4 Interpolation

You can insert words into the quotation so that it reads more clearly. Use square brackets.

'the lesser three [castles] were destroyed, leaving Oxayama, which commanded the entire Bizen plain, as the headquarters of the daimyoi of Bizen' (Scheiner 1974: 111).

A reference list: some examples

The following are examples of the Harvard System of referencing different kinds of books, articles and other material. Use them as a guide. Other referencing systems follow the same basic principles. You provide the same details, but the setting out may be different. Check which system is required. If you come across an example that is not covered below, use your own judgement. There are no rigid rules. Be as thorough and as consistent as you can. Arrange your reference list or bibliography alphabetically by author. Write the author's name as it appears in the book or article. Don't for example, abbreviate Smith, John Peter to Smith, J.P.

A book:

>Anderson, Paul
>1976   Elementary Physics. Chicago: University of Chicago
>   Press.

(A typical book. Note that the title is underlined and that the place of publication is a *city* — Chicago.)

An article:

>Appleyard, Peter
>1976   'Labour Costs and Profit Margins', The Australian
>   Journal of Management, 24, 2(June): 24–68.

(A typical article. Note that the actual title of the journal is underlined, but you don't provide publication details. Indicate the article title by the quotation marks. The 24 refers to the volume number and the 2 to the second number or issue of that volume, which came out in June. You also provide page numbers.)

Other examples:

> Abrahams, Isaac and Bailey, William
> 1975   Essays on the Political Economy of Asia. New York: Monthly Review Press.
> (Two authors of a book. Write them in the order in which they appear on the title page.)
>
> Australian Bureau of Statistics
> 1976   Birth Expectations of Married Women. Canberra: ABS.
> (A government publication. Note the abbreviation ABS.)
>
> Australian Government Publishing Service
> 1978   Style Manual for Authors, Editors and Printers of Australian Government Publications. 3rd. ed. Canberra: AGPS.
> (Notice where to place the edition. Most books have only one edition. A new edition means that changes have been made. Ignore reprinting, which is simply more copies of the original.)
>
> Baxter, Peter and Samuels, John (eds.)
> 1972   Morality and the Scientist: Selected Readings. Dublin: University of Dublin Press.
> (A book edited by two authors. It contains a number of articles by different people.)
>
> Brown, John Smith and Ward, Robert.
> 1982   An Introduction to Psychology. Ringwood, Victoria: Thomas Nelson.
> (If your publishing centre is a small town or village, give further details — Victoria in this case. An exception is Harmondsworth, which is very well known in the publishing world.)
>
> Carmody, John and others
> 1984   Aspects of Modern Business Management. Chicago: University of Chicago Press.
> (Usually if there are more than two authors, you don't write down all the names. You may also write it like this: Carmody, J. *et al.* Latin for 'and others'.)

Fest, Joachim C.
1970 The Face of the Third Reich. Translated from the German by Michael Bullock. London: Weidenfeld & Nicholson.
(Give the name of the person who does the translation.)

1981 'Investment Demand Grows in Australia'. Weekend Australian. 11–12 February: 24–28.
(A newspaper article with no author named. Notice the setting out.)

Irwin, George
1982 'Hawke's Future', Canberra Times, 21 January: 62.
(A newspaper article with an author.)

Kiernan, Thomas
1985 'Economic Measurement', in Frank Tyler (ed), Principles of Economics: Selected Readings. London: Clark Books: 24–36.
(An article in a collection edited by Tyler. In your essay you will reference as Kiernan 1985. The book will be catalogued under Tyler's name. Note that you give page numbers when you refer to a specific article in a collection.)

Long, John
1979 Fertility Rates in African Women, paper presented to the Annual Meeting of the American Political Science Association, New York, 30 May–1 June.
(An unpublished conference paper. You do not underline unpublished works.)

Murphy, Eamon
1977 'Labour Organisations in the Cotton Mills of Tamilnad, 1918–1939', Ph.D Thesis, Department of History, University of Western Australia.
(An unpublished thesis)

National Population Inquiry
1975 First Report: Population and Australia: A Demographic Analysis and Projection. Canberra: AGPS.

1978 Supplementary Report: Population and Australia: Recent Demographic Trends and their Implications. Canberra: AGPS.

(Note the setting out of two works by the same author, the National Population Inquiry.)

Smith, John F.
1984 Interview, Perth, 25 August.
(An interview.)

Smith, Peter
1985 Lecture, Chemistry 111. University of Sydney.
(A lecture.)

Srivastava, R.
1978a 'Shifting Cultivation in India', Man in India, 57, 4: 331–344.

1978b 'Cultural Factors in Development Process'. Journal of Peasant Studies, 7, 2: 213–233.

(Two works published by the same person in the same year. Reference like this: According to Srivastava (1978a), Indian peasants . . . .)

Tayal, Maureen
1977 'Indian Indentured Labour in Natal, 1890–1911', The Indian Economic and Social History Review, XIV, 4, (Oct-Dec): 519–548.

(Note the use of the Roman numerals XIV for 14. Some journals still retain this form. Copy what appears on the title page.)

Tobin, Peter
1985 Review of J.R. Smith, Sociology. Perth: Longman Cheshire, 1980 in The Australian Sociologist, 19, 4 (August): 410.
(A book review.)

10 Book Reviews

A book review expresses the reviewer's opinion about the quality or worth of a book. It is, therefore, a **subjective** evaluation. Book reviews can be inaccurate, shallow, unfair, or even very nasty. When reading a review, therefore, ask yourself:

- Does the reviewer justify his or her opinions, or simply make assertions?
- Does the reviewer judge the book according to the author's aims or according to how the reviewer would have approached the subject?

Writing a review is relatively easy; writing a book can take a lifetime of hard work: there are many more reviewers than there are authors.

An academic book review generally:

- Describes the book. Gives a summary of its contents.
- Says something about the author and her or his qualifications to write the book.

- Comments on the appearance, organisation, layout and style.
- Evaluates the scholarship, particularly the accuracy of the data and the quality of the argument.
- Compares it with other books in the same field.

Most tertiary students neglect book reviews, yet reviews can be extremely useful. Secondary school students can also learn much from reading and analysing reviews.

The value of book reviews

1 They provide a quick summary.

- Dr Smith's monograph is a major contribution to the study of eighteenth century scientific thought. Smith argues that . . . .
- *Psycho-cybernetics* is, in essence, an account of . . .
- It is a useful book for the student of Australian fiscal problems.
- The central theme of the book is . . . .

2 They let the reader know for whom the book will be suitable.

- *Elementary Physics* is a very simple textbook, particularly suitable for lower secondary school students. It presents, in a clear and simple style, some of . . . .
- This detailed and difficult account is written for the expert in the field.

3 They tell you something about the author.

- Professor Brown is one of the world's leading experts on the use of computers in schools. She was trained . . . .
- Dr James was a research officer for Mr Peacock, and is still a prominent member of the Liberal Party.
- This book is based on Paul Morrison's doctoral dissertation for Moscow University.

4 They help you keep up with new information, theories and debates.

- This book provides a wealth of information on recent developments in caring for the aged.
- Watson's approach is entirely new.
- My own findings on the issue do not agree . . . .
- Ann Hubbard's analysis makes full use of the latest methods of . . . .

5 They help develop your ability and confidence to criticise academic writing. You can learn what to look for when analysing a book.

- His sources are out-of-date and largely limited to American Studies.
- It is surprising that Malcolm Lyall has ignored the statistics kept by the central government.
- O'Brien at no stage satisfactorily defines the terms 'tradition' and 'modernity'.
- This work is written in such a turgid style that its argument becomes incomprehensible.
- It is a brilliant account, spoilt by . . .
- It is inexplicable that a work claiming to be a history of linguistics should not take account of the recent studies of . . .
- An extraordinary book! Peter Frank achieves the remarkable feat of making one of the most exciting episodes in British history seem like a vicar's tea-party.
- The author launches an acrimonious attack on other experts in this specialised field.

Keep in mind, however, that reviewers can be wrong, bigoted and unfair. Often the review will tell you as much about the reviewer as about the book.

How to locate a book review

You will find most book reviews in **serials**. Sometimes called **periodicals**, these are publications (newspapers, journals, bulletins or magazines) that are issued at regular periods or intervals (such as daily, weekly, monthly, or

Book Reviews

yearly). While you will find book reviews in good quality newspapers such as *The Times Literary Supplement*, your most likely source will be journals, especially those relating to a particular discipline (astronomy, psychology, inorganic chemistry, history and so on). To locate a book review with the minimum effort, you need to know which sources in your library list them. As I've said before, learning how to use your library is one of the first and most important skills you should acquire.

You have three main ways of locating a review:

1 Through Book Review Indexes

A book review index is simply an alphabetical list by author and title of all the books reviewed in the journals which the index covers. The index specifies the particular issue of the journal carrying the review so that you can locate it in the library.

Some book review indexes contain **general** lists of reviews drawn from many different subject areas (such as the humanities, science, social sciences). Particularly useful are:

> *Book Review Digest* (summarises some reviews)
> *Book Review Index*
> *Choice* (prints reviews)
> *Australian Book Reviews*

2. Through Indexing and Abstracting Journals

These journals list book reviews as well as the articles published in the many journals in their field. Ask a librarian for help in choosing the most likely index. Some possibilities are:

> *Science Citation Index*
> *Social Sciences Citation Index*
> *APAIS* (Australian Public Affairs Information Service)
> *Business Periodicals Index*
> *Social Sciences Index*
> *Humanities Index*

Book review indexes save you a great deal of time. You can find out who reviewed a book, and where the review was

151

published. Often you can find a number of reviews quite quickly. There are, however, some problems with book review indexes:

- Some relevant journals may not be covered. You may have to do some detective work to find reviews that are in journals that are not in the indexes you are using.
- There is sometimes a time-lag between the publication of the book and a review of it, as well as a time-lag between publication of the review and its appearance in an index.
- Not every library will hold the general book review indexes.
- Some indexes are very complicated, and you may need help to use them. While most librarians are very helpful, they are often very busy, and you may have trouble in getting help. If you have difficulty talking to a particular librarian, try again when the library is not too busy or another librarian is on duty. Or ask the library to give you and the other students in your class a brief introduction to using indexes.

However, despite these limitations, you should learn as soon as possible how to use book review indexes. If your book was published in 1976, for example, start off by consulting the book review index (or indexes) for that year and then for the following years (1977, etc). You will find that most reviews will appear within three years after the book has been published, but sometimes it may be quite a few years later.

Besides using the book review indexes you can also locate reviews by:

3 Browsing through journals on the library shelves

Browsing can be a very inefficient way of locating book reviews. This method, however, has certain advantages:

- By browsing you will very quickly get some idea of the subject coverage of journals as well as seeing what books are reviewed. If you are not looking for a review of a particular book, browsing is an excellent way of finding out what is being written in your field.

Book Reviews

- The latest journals can be particularly rewarding. You may even be the first person in your class to read about an important new work. (If you are interested in 'game-playing', you can use this information to good advantage: most lecturers are very impressed with students who have read the latest reviews.)

Make your browsing more efficient by first consulting the list of journals held by your library. Note down the journals that seem to be relevant to your subject. (Your course outline, essay reading list and tutorial reading list may also give you the titles of useful journals.)

You will also discover that most journals print an index (often in the last issue of the year) to all the reviews and articles that have appeared in the journal either for that year or for a longer period. Book reviews are extremely useful when you are reading for a tutorial or for an essay. The review will help you read a book more effectively, so long as you don't accept uncritically everything the reviewer writes. Students who use reviews usually gain the reputation of being particularly keen and informed. Reviews will also help you find books that are worth reading. For both practical and more idealistic reasons, therefore, you should get into the habit of regularly reading book reviews: you will achieve more with less effort if you do.

Writing a book review

Many undergraduate courses, especially at second- and third-year level, will require you to write a review. Approach the book in a systematic fashion:

- Read the contents page to learn not only what the book is about but also what the author sees as important.
- The Preface (or Foreword) and Introduction will usually tell you about the author and his or her purpose, approach and methods. Note, in particular, the author's account of how the book took shape. The Index may also be a valuable guide to the contents of the book.
- Read the last chapter carefully. Has the author achieved what he or she set out to do? Have the questions been answered convincingly?

- Skim the rest of the book, concentrating where necessary on the important sections. Always read the first and last paragraphs of each chapter with care; they usually contain the essence of the chapter.
- Examine the bibliography critically. Has the author referred to recent publications? Is there a variety of sources? Has the author made good use of the sources?
- Consider the style. Is the book well written? If you found the book difficult to understand, was it because of the topic or the expression?
- Use the reviews in a journal in the same field as a guide to format. Be fair. Mention the book's strengths as well as its weaknesses. Be critical but balanced. It is far easier to criticise than to write a book!

What to put in your review:
- Begin with full bibliographical details: author, full title, place of publication. publisher, date of publication, edition (if second or later), price (if known).
- Say something about the general appearance and layout. Is it either unusually good or bad? Is the print difficult to read? Are the margins too narrow? If it has diagrams, maps and illustrations, consider whether they are clear and useful. Does it have an accurate and comprehensive index? Check by tracing a few entries.
- Say something about the author. Is he or she qualified to write the book? The book jacket, foreword or introduction may give you relevant details.
- Comment on the value of the book. Say for whom the book is suitable: experts, students etc.
- Say what the book is about. Provide a *brief* summary.
- Compare it with other books of the same kind. If it is a revised edition, try to compare it with the earlier edition.
- Comment critically on the methodology, content, conclusions.
- Comment upon the style. Is it easy to read? Does it flow? Is the style suitable for the audience for whom the book is intended?
- Look at the book's bibliography. Is it up-to-date?

Further Reading

The following are a few of the huge number of general references on writing skills. There are also a huge number of specialised books for specific subjects such as business communication and scientific writing. To find them, use the subject headings in the card catalogue.

Anderson, Jonathan and others
1970 <u>Thesis and Assignment Writing</u>. Sydney: John Wiley.
(Provides general advice on assignment writing. Chapter 9 is particularly helpful on setting out tables and figures.)

Australian Government Publishing Service
1978 <u>Style Manual for Authors, Editors and Printers of Australian Government Publications</u>. 3rd ed. Canberra: AGPS.
(A mine of information on many topics: lists of abbreviations, symbols, foreign currency symbols, etc. Very good on government publications, reports and legal papers.)

Bailey, R
1984 <u>A Survival Kit for Writing English</u>. 2nd ed. Melbourne: Longman Cheshire.
(A concise introduction to punctuation and grammar, especially for students taking English courses.)

Baker, Sheridan
1977 <u>The Practical Stylist</u>. 4th ed. New York: Thomas Y. Crowell.
(A detailed book on all aspects of writing.)

Clanchy, John and Ballard, Brigid
1981 <u>Essay Writing for Students: A Guide for Arts and Social Science Students</u>. Melbourne: Longman Cheshire.
(A comprehensive guide.)

Fowler, Henry Watson
1965 A Dictionary of Modern English Usage. 2nd ed.
 Revised by Sir Ernest Gowers. Oxford: Clarendon Press.
 (The bible!)

Gowers, Sir Ernest Arthur
1973 The Complete Plain Words. 2nd ed. Harmondsworth:
 Penguin.
(Classic work on how to write; immensely readable; especially good on writing clearly.)

Lindsay, John
1984 A Guide to Scientific Writing. Melbourne: Longman
 Cheshire.
(Explains how to present logical arguments that are easy to read and fully scientific.)

Marshall, Lorraine A. and Rowland, Frances,
1981 A Guide to Learning Independently. Melbourne:
 Longman Cheshire.
(A general guide to adjusting to tertiary study. Contains very useful chapters on assignments, scientific and report writing.)

Millward, Celia
1980 Handbook for Writers. New York: Holt Rinehart and
 Winston.
(Detailed guide to grammar, punctuation, using words and developing an argument.)

Strunk, W. Jr. and White, E.B.
1972 The Elements of Style. 2nd ed. New York:
 Macmillan.
(Brief introduction to topic and structure, language and writing, style.)